The Chartered
Institute of Marketing

CIM Companion:

marketing research and information

CIM Publishing

CIM Publishing

The Chartered Institute of Marketing
Moor Hall
Cookham
Berkshire
SL6 9QH

www.cim.co.uk

First published 2003
© CIM Publishing 2003

Series Editors: John Ling and Mark Stuart

It is the publisher's policy to use paper manufactured from sustainable forests.

British Library Cataloguing in Publication Data
A CIP catalogue record for this book can be obtained from the British Library.

ISBN 0 902130 80 3

Printed and bound by The Cromwell Press, Trowbridge, Wiltshire.
Cover design by Marie-Claire Bonhommet.

contents

Study guide

This Companion is written to complement the recommended core text for this subject, *Marketing Research – an Integrated Approach*, Alan Wilson, FT Prentice-Hall, 2003. It aims to offer you support as either an individual or group learner as you move along the road to becoming a competent and proficient marketer. This is a process of learning that has two important elements:

Understanding marketing concepts and their application

The study text in the following Sessions has been written to highlight the concepts that you will need to grasp as you start to understand the principles of marketing research, what marketing research can achieve, and how its findings can be used. The material is described briefly and concisely to enable you to cover a range of key material relating to marketing research. It does not attempt to be fully comprehensive and you should read widely from other sources. To develop your understanding of the concepts introduced here, your reading should include:

- Recommended course texts (readings are shown in Table 2 for each of the Sessions in this book).

- The marketing press and quality national newspapers.

- More comprehensive marketing textbooks (detailed on the module reading list in the syllabus), which provide a wider context for the concepts explained in this Companion, and more Case Studies and examples to illustrate strategic and operational marketing in practice.

Developing the skills to implement marketing activity

Equally important in the journey towards marketing excellence is the acquisition, development and refining of a range of skills that are required by marketers across all industries and sectors. These transferable skills hold the key to the effective implementation of the marketing techniques explored in this book.

Using the Companion

You should familiarise yourself with the syllabus for this module, which is shown in Appendix 2. In this Companion it has been broken down into fifteen Sessions, each of which covers approximately the same proportion of the content. Every student brings with them to their studies different levels of experience – as a customer, from previous studies, or from working in marketing or sales. You should therefore be aware that whilst you may need to spend considerable time

1

on unfamiliar areas of the syllabus, you can usually make up this time when studying other areas with which you are more familiar.

Each Session has a series of short activities, which you should try to complete as you work your way through the text. These will help you to check your understanding of the material, and brief feedback is provided at the end of each Session so that you can compare your answers. Some of these are exam questions from past papers, so you can use them to help practise your exam technique.

Each Session also contains a Case Study and a series of related questions. Try to complete these without reference to your notes, or the Session text, and then compare your answers with some key points given at the end of the Companion in Appendix 1.

At the end of each Session you will also find a number of projects. These are designed to help you extend and apply your understanding of the subjects covered in the Session. These often take the form of practical activities undertaken in your own organisation or an organisation of your choice. Whilst not all participants in CIM programmes work in an organisation, these projects can still provide valuable learning if interpreted rather than followed to the letter, or if applied to organisations that you are aware of.

Finally, you will see that there is a specimen exam paper in Appendix 3. This can help you with your revision, exam technique and preparation. Nearer to your actual exam, allow time to complete the paper under exam conditions – that is, allow three hours of uninterrupted time, and complete the paper without reference to your notes or the study material. When you have completed the exercise, you can compare your answers to the notes in Appendix 4. If either your approach to the exercise or the comparison of your answers highlight areas of particular weakness, you should refer back to the text and reread the relevant Session, together with the chapters of the supporting textbook.

This Companion's structure and content follows the syllabus order, as this module follows a standard "process" which in itself is logical in its "flow".

Table 1 – Key skills

	Using ICT and the Internet	Using financial information and metrics	Presenting information	Working with others	Applying business law	Improving and developing own learning	Problem solving
Session 1	Project C		1.1 1.2	1.2		Project activities	Case Study
Session 2			2.1 2.2	Project B		Project activities	Case Study
Session 3	3.1		Project B	Project C	Case Study	Project activities	Case Study
Session 4	4.2 Projects		4.3	Projects A & B		Project activities	Case Study
Session 5	5.1 Projects A & B		5.3	Project C		Project activities	Case Study
Session 6			6.1	Projects A & B		Project activities	Case Study
Session 7			7.1 Case Study	Projects A & B	Project C	Project activities	Case Study
Session 8	Projects B & C		8.1 8.2	Project A		Project activities	Case Study
Session 9		9.2	9.1	Project A		Project activities	Case Study
Session 10	10.1 Project C		10.1	Project A		Project activities	Case Study
Session 11			11.1 11.2 Project A	Projects B & C		Project activities	Case Study
Session 12			12.1 12.2 Projects B & C	Project C		Project activities	Case Study
Session 13	Project C	13.1 Case Study	13.2	Projects A & B		Project activities	Case Study
Session 14		14.1	14.2 Case Study	Projects A, B & C		Project activities	Case Study
Session 15		Case Study	15.1 15.2 Case Study	Projects A & C		Project activities	Case Study

Table 2 – Web sites

www.cim.co.uk	The Chartered Institute of Marketing.
www.connectedinmarketing.com	Everything you need to know about e-marketing.
www.cimvirtualinstitute.com	Key learning tool for CIM students.
www.adslogans.co.uk	Online database of advertising slogans, enabling marketers to check whether a slogan is already in use.
www.ipa.co.uk	Institute of Practitioners in Advertising.
www.asa.org.uk	Advertising Standards Agency.
www.spca.org.uk	The Marketing Communications Consultants Association.
www.isp.org.uk	The Institute of Sales Promotion.
www.ppa.co.uk	Periodical Publishers Association.
www.adassoc.org.uk	Advertising Association.
www.new-marketing.org	Cranfield research updates into new marketing issues, customer segmentation, and the repercussions for the marketing practitioner.
www.e-bulletin.com	Guide to exhibitions, events and resources.
www.venuefinder.com	International venue and event suppliers' directory.
www.europa.eu.int	European Union online.
www.wapforum.org	Industry Association responsible for creating the standards for WAP (Wireless Application Protocol), now called the Open Mobile Alliance.
www.prnewswire.co.uk	UK media monitoring service – reviews mentions in all media types (print, online publications and broadcast).
www.keynote.co.uk	Market research reports.
www.verdict.co.uk	Retail research reports.
www.datamonitor.com	Market analysis providing global data collection and in-depth analysis across any industry.
www.store.eiu.com	Economist Intelligence Unit, providing country-specific global business analysis.
www.mintel.com	Consumer market research.
www.royalmail.co.uk	General marketing advice and information.

www.ft.com	Financial Times online newspaper and archives (subscription based).
www.afxpress.com	Business news plus industry trends.
www.statistics.gov.uk	Detailed information on a variety of consumer demographics from the UK Government Statistics Office.
www.accountingweb.co.uk	Provides the latest financial news, company information, taxation guides and other financial matters.
www.financewise.com	Specialist index of web sites providing links to information on all aspects of finance (registration required).
http://web.utk.edu/~jwachowi/wacho_world.html	Exhaustive listing of web financial resources presented with a student perspective.
www.bized.ac.uk	Contains a complete example of a company called Cameron Balloons, complete with finances. Can be used to illustrate all the basic principles of financial decisions made in this Companion.
www.amazon.co.uk	Classic example of groundbreaking online customer service and marketing orientation in practice.
www.johnsonandjohnson.com	An example of a "credo" and its documented influence on the activities of this global corporation.
www.mckinseyquarterly.com	Free full text articles on strategy issues from one of the world's premier business journals.
www.strategy-business.com	Online journal on the topic of business strategy, with good search facilities.
www.virgin.com	A well known successful example of unrelated diversification.
www.cbi.org.uk/innovation/index.html	Information on innovation in industry.
www.brandrepublic.com	Useful notes on the preparation of marketing plans, and access to research data.
www.hbsp.harvard.edu	Free abstracts from Harvard Business Review articles.

Table 3 – Background reading

The following references are suggested background readings for each Session. It is suggested that you undertake this reading before studying the relevant Companion Session.

Session	Reading from core text: Alan Wilson, *Marketing Research: an Integrated Approach* (2003), FT Prentice-Hall. **Robin J Birn, *The International Handbook of Market Research Techniques* (2nd Edition), Kogan Page**
Session 1	Chapter 1 – The role of marketing research and customer information in decision making.
Session 2	Chapter 1 – The role of marketing research and customer information in decision making.
Session 3	Chapter 3 – Secondary data and customer databases.
Session 4	Chapter 3 – Secondary data and customer databases.
Session 5	Chapter 2 – The marketing research process. **Chapter 5 – Questionnaire design.**
Session 6	Chapter 2 – The marketing research process. **Chapter 1 – Planning market research surveys.**
Session 7	Chapter 2 – The marketing research process.
Session 8	Chapter 3 – Secondary data and customer databases. **Chapter 2 – Desk research.**
Session 9	Chapter 4 – Collecting observation data. Chapter 5 – Collecting and analysing qualitative data. Chapter 6 – Collecting quantitative data. **Chapter 6 – Geo-demographics.**
Session 10	Chapter 4 – Collecting observation data.
Session 11	Chapter 5 – Collecting and analysing qualitative data. Chapter 6 – Collecting quantitative data. **Chapters 8-23 – Data collection.**
Session 12	Chapter 7 – Designing questionnaires. **Chapter 5 – Questionnaire design.**
Session 13	Chapter 8 – Sampling methods. **Chapter 3 – Standards and methods.** **Chapter 4 – Sampling and statistics.**
Session 14	Chapter 9 – Analysing quantitative data. **Chapters 24-30 – Analysis and modelling.**
Session 15	Chapter 10 – Presenting the research results. **Chapter 31 – Presentations and report writing.**

Table 4 – Marketing models

The text in the Companion Sessions refers to appropriate models, but does not reproduce these as they can be seen in the core textbook, *Marketing Research: An Integrated Approach* by Alan Wilson. References for the models used in this core textbook are supplied in the following table. Please note that these do not necessarily represent the full range of models that you will need to study for your exam or assessment.

Session	Marketing Model	Reference
Session 1	■ Information providers.	■ Page 12
Session 2	■ No specific models.	
Session 3	■ No specific models.	
Session 4	■ A flowchart for evaluating secondary data.	■ Page 54
Session 5	■ The marketing research process. ■ Contents of research proposal.	■ Page 21 ■ Page 28
Session 6	■ No specific models.	
Session 7	■ No specific models.	
Session 8	■ No specific models.	
Session 9	■ Example discussion guide.	■ Page 103
Session 10	■ No specific models.	
Session 11	■ Classification of survey methods.	■ Page 122
Session 12	■ Two-way communication. ■ Questionnaire design process. ■ Examples of Likert Scale items. ■ Semantic differential profile. ■ Funnel sequence of questioning.	■ Page 146 ■ Page 147 ■ Page 160 ■ Page 162 ■ Page 169
Session 13	■ The sampling process. ■ Normal distribution graph.	■ Page 176 ■ Page 190
Session 14	■ No specific models.	
Session 15	■ Audience's thinking process. ■ Doughnut chart. ■ Line graph. ■ Bar chart. ■ Stacked bar chart. ■ Pictogram.	■ Page 233 ■ Page 241 ■ Page 242 ■ Page 243 ■ Page 243 ■ Page 243

Session 1

The role of information in marketing

Introduction

This Session introduces the whole module and considers the role that information plays in the overall marketing process. It considers the types of decisions marketers are involved in making, and how information can help with such decisions. Finally, it looks at the concept of knowledge management and the role this plays in business today.

LEARNING OUTCOMES

At the end of this Session you will be able to:

- Demonstrate a broad appreciation of the need for information in marketing management.

- Describe the role of information in the overall marketing process.

- Explain the concept of knowledge management and its importance in a knowledge-based economy.

The role of information in marketing decision making

Collecting and analysing information is a key process for marketing management. It aids problem solving and is the raw material for making improvements in products and services to reflect changing customer needs. It facilitates marketing management overall by reducing the uncertainty and risk associated with making decisions.

A marketing-orientated organisation looks outwards to the business environment to take advantage of opportunities and to minimise threats.

Internal information can assist in objective setting by providing an informed analysis of performance to date, and by identifying the strengths of the organisation and any potential weaknesses that need to be addressed. External information can assist in taking advantage of the potential opportunities and in developing strategies to combat the potential threats to future business success.

The **marketing audit** is a systematic investigation of the internal and external environment, alongside which organisations may instigate research into particular internal functions and special areas of interest externally.

Here is a checklist of the areas most likely to be examined.

Internal Audit	External Audit
Operating results Sales. Market share. Profit margins. Costs. **Strategic issues** Marketing objectives. Market segmentation. Competitive advantage. Core competences. Positioning. Portfolio analysis. **Marketing mix effectiveness** Product. Price. Promotion. Distribution. **Marketing structures** Marketing organisation. Marketing training. Intra-and interdepartmental. Communications. **Marketing systems** Marketing information system. Marketing planning system. Marketing control system.	**Macroenvironment** Economic: inflation, interest rates and unemployment. Social/Cultural: lifestyle and attitudes. Technological: new products and materials. Political/Legal: new laws, regulations and monopolies. Ecological: conservation, pollution and energy. **The market** Market size: growth rates, trends and developments. Customers: profiles, behaviour. Market segmentation: customer groupings. Distribution: power changes, channel attractiveness, influencers. **Competition** Who are the major competitors, actual and potential? What are their objectives and strategies? What are their strengths and weaknesses? Market share and size of competitors. Profitability analysis. Entry barriers.

Source: *Principles & Practice of Marketing,* David Jobber, 2001, McGraw-Hill.

The information from these audits informs the marketing planning process and the action planning of the marketing function. Long term and day-to-day decisions are made about priorities for the marketing strategy and mix. Decisions have financial, production and human resource implications, so the more accurate the information the more likely decisions can be made with confidence and reduced risk.

Information for marketing planning

There are many different planning frameworks used in marketing and information gathering. You may be gathering primary or secondary information (the former is new whereas the latter already exists), but a framework is useful because it gives a structure to your activity.

One such framework is as follows:

1. Overview and context.

2. The marketing audit – Analysis of the external marketplace and business environment.
   Internal analysis of the current marketing activities and brand image.
   Analysis of the competitive position.

3. Segmentation and target markets, customer relationships and buying behaviour.

4. Marketing objectives.

5. Strategic choices for products and markets.

6. Marketing mix – Product.
   Price.
   Place.
   Promotion.
   People.
   Process.
   Physical evidence.
   Periodicity.

7. Action planning for implementation.

8. Control and budgets.

Looking at each stage in turn:

1. Overview and context

At this stage the planner would look at last year's plan (secondary data) and assess where the organisation is now against where it planned to be, to help put this year's plan into context.

2. The marketing audit

This stage involves a full analysis of the situation at the time – the "where are we now?" phase of the planning process. It involves looking at information held in the Marketing Information System (see Session 2), and taking key information into a SWOT analysis. Most of this information will be secondary data, but some primary research may be undertaken into customer perceptions.

3. Segmentation and target markets, customer relationships and buying behaviour

Customer profiling will be undertaken from existing records, and customer research carried out to check our understanding of buying behaviour in target markets.

4. Marketing objectives

We may look back at last year's performance to review what was achieved and what lessons can be learnt.

5. Strategic choices for products and markets

Again, analysis of current data will be undertaken – portfolio analysis, market attractiveness/business strength etc., to make more informed decisions about strategic options.

6. The marketing mix

This is where research can be particularly useful. For example, it can help us answer the following questions:

Product
What new products do we need to develop?
Which new product developments will work? Which will fail?
What new products is technology making possible?

Which packaging will be most attractive to our customers and most practical for our products?
How should our brands be positioned/repositioned?

Price

How should we price our products?
How should we respond to our competitors' changes in pricing?
How do our customers perceive our prices?
How important is price to our customers when selecting a brand?

Place

Which channel will be best to get our products to our customers?
Should we be expanding our channels?
How do our channel members feel about us?
Can we afford to expand?
Which locations will be best to reach our customers?
Should we be selling online, and what impact will that have on our existing channel members?

Promotion

Who should we target?
What should the message be?
How should we reach them (channels to be used)?
How much budget should we allocate to our promotions?
What is the best promotional mix to reach our target customers?
How will our target customers perceive a particular message?
What style of advertising will be best, and which media should we use?
Are we reaching the right group of customers?
How effective was our last campaign?

People

How do our customers perceive our staff?
What do customers think about our level of service?
How suitable is our mix of staffing – part-time and full-time?
How will our staff feel about a particular style/colour of uniform?

Process

How well are our customer processes working?
What do our customers think?
How can we improve processes?

Physical evidence

How well is our logo/brand image recognised?
How do our customers perceive our image?
Do we need to update our image?

Periodicity

When is it best to launch new products?
When should campaigns be launched?
How many seasons does our product have?
Do we celebrate special occasions such as Christmas?

7. **Action planning for implementation**

At this stage we may need to check competitor activity before scheduling ours.

8. **Control and budgets**

What budget is available?
How can progress be monitored?
Finally, we need to schedule in post-testing for promotional activity, and measurement through internal records and follow-up research.

The above highlights how valuable both existing (or secondary information) and primary research (collected first hand) can be to the marketing planning process.

Activity 1.1

For an organisation of your choice, explain how information resulting from marketing research forms part of the marketing audit.

What is knowledge management?

Knowledge management refers to the way organisations develop, keep, and use their intellectual capital. Intellectual capital can be drawn from a number of sources, for example:

- Their people.

- Their customers.

- Their information systems.

Articles and books on knowledge management often tend to focus on one particular aspect of knowledge management, such as developing customer information systems or a learning culture.

Just as with our own memories, if we are to use knowledge effectively we need to have a way of:

- Capturing and developing knowledge that is valuable.
- Being able to store knowledge effectively.
- Being able to retrieve and use knowledge effectively.

Over the last 20 years businesses have started to value the knowledge "held" both in printed media, technologically and orally within organisations. Information can be valuable not just because it can lead to a major competitive advantage over the competition, but because it can also aid organisational, individual and product development. In the next section we look at the importance of retaining and using knowledge or intellectual capital within organisations.

Barriers to developing intellectual capital

Most organisations have lots of opportunities to develop their human or information systems capital, but often they are either passed by or deemed too expensive to exploit.

Figure 1.1: Examples of barriers to developing intellectual capital

Barrier	Example	Consequence
Time and cost.	Training courses are cancelled at the last minute because workloads are deemed too great and there is no short-term impact on the business.	■ Development is regarded as a luxury not a necessity. ■ Workforce skills become more and more outdated.

| Lack of knowledge of what is available. | The customer data collected at point of sale is not analysed or used. | ■ Customer needs are not understood or satisfied.
■ Competitors are able to gain competitive advantage by using their own data. |
| Undervaluing internal knowledge. | Marketing strategy is developed in head office without consulting customer contact staff. | ■ Valuable organisation-specific knowledge is ignored in favour of generally available market analysis.
■ Organisation loses its competitive advantage. |

Barriers to keeping intellectual capital

Even where intellectual capital is identified and developed, much of it can be lost or become useless if it is not actively used and kept up to date.

Figure 1.2: Examples of barriers to keeping intellectual capital

Barrier	Example	Consequence
Loss of people outside the organisation or department.	Staff are retired early as part of a cost cutting plan.	■ Important files of information are shredded as no one understands their contents. ■ The intellectual capital of a generation of staff is lost to the organisation for good.
Lack of effective storage.	Useful information from a product launch is captured by individual team members, but is not stored for wider and future use.	■ The organisation does not improve its skills at as fast a rate as it could do.

Outdated systems.	Key customer knowledge is captured on a database, but when the software is updated the database is not moved over to the new system.	■ Valuable marketing information is squandered. ■ The organisation loses out to a competitor who is able to spot an emerging trend that was only visible in the data that was lost.

Barriers to using intellectual capital

Having and storing knowledge is insufficient if it cannot be either brought to the attention of, or accessed by, those that need it, when they need it. This can be one of the most challenging areas for an organisation to overcome.

Figure 1.3: Examples of barriers to using intellectual capital

Barrier	Example	Consequence
Overwhelmed.	Key information needs to be extracted from pages and pages of data and management information reports.	■ Information is never used, so the organisation gains no value from it. ■ Eventually the information stops being stored altogether.
Poor marketing.	Detailed product costing information is not seen by salespeople, as they do not know of its existence.	■ Sales do not understand some of the consequences of their customer negotiations. ■ Organisational profitability is reduced.

Limited access.	Customer database can only be interrogated by IT specialists after a one month delay.	■ Decisions are taken on dated information, as the information is not available in a timely fashion.
Secrecy.	Competitor information is kept by the PR department, as they believe this increases their perceived value to the organisation.	■ Product managers do not gain access to key information that would help them increase profitability.

A knowledge management programme might include some of the following activities:

■ Develop global knowledge strategies.

■ Design knowledge events.

■ Support knowledge change initiatives.

■ Review knowledge systems.

■ Develop individual knowledge capability.

■ Create people policies for knowledge workers.

■ Deliver knowledge workshops.

Some organisations have now started to gather "stories" about projects they have undertaken, making video clips of those involved talking about what happened, and then inserting these clips into an online database that is available and searchable on the company's Intranet.

Activity 1.2

The questions below will help you to think through what type of "knowledge management" is available within your own organisation and how well it is organised for retrieval.

1.   What is your organisation's definition of knowledge management?

---

2.   Do you have an existing knowledge management strategy?

3.   Where is knowledge to be found in your organisation?

4.   Where can you find outside knowledge about your organisation?

5.   What do you want to do with your organisation's knowledge?

6.   What knowledge is the most/least important to your organisation?

7.   Which knowledge is the easiest/hardest to manage?

8.   Who manages knowledge in your organisation?

Write a short report about the types of information being "lost" in your organisation and the potential value of such knowledge to the development of the organisation.

Case Study

The fast track to success

Metro's marketing strategy pulls new readers and advertisers

Metro (London) was launched in 1999 amid rumours that the Modern Times group was planning a free newspaper launch in London. Associated Newspapers was eager to defend its position in the London market and research showed that 400,000 frequent tube users were not reading a national newspaper. The challenge was to reach this lucrative niche, without cannibalising the sale of Associated's other newspaper brands. Metro is the sixth largest newspaper in the UK and the world's largest free newspaper.

Advertising initiatives

Metro's sales team was set up to mirror the structure of an advertising agency. The newspaper was sold to agencies as a "media moment" competing for attention against radio and outdoor, rather than pitching as a traditional newspaper.

'We gave agencies first-hand evidence of the Metro phenomenon every weekday by taking them to Waterloo station and allowing them to experience a "Metro",' explains Karen Wall, Marketing Manager of Metro UK. 'From an elevated balcony every morning you can witness an entire "sea of blue" created from the hundreds of blue front-page mastheads.'

Metro quickly secured some long-term advertising deals covering a host of market sectors, including retail, motoring, travel, finance and dotcoms. MMS shows that from launch, Metro London has taken £40 million of national display advertising revenue (YTD December 2000).

Building on success

The phenomenal success of Metro in London led to the formula being quickly rolled out across the country into key urban centres, launching "Britain's First Urban National" newspaper.

Research showed that there were over 8 million adults living outside London who were working and not reading a national daily newspaper. Profiling these adults revealed that they were likely to be young and affluent – Metro's core target audience.

Next, Metro readers in London were profiled using MOSAIC geodemographics. National research shows that Metro is read by a young, urbanite audience, as they commute to work in the morning. Seventy per cent of readers are ABC1, 77% are aged 16-44, and 81% of readers work. Research also revealed that many of Metro's audience never read or were lapsed readers of national newspapers, making them highly sought after by advertisers.

Brand development

Two separate organisations were appointed to work on its brand positioning and essence. Throughout the year a clear, consistent message was delivered to the industry using Case Studies, media exposure, direct mail, and through launching an online media-pack site www.metro.co.uk/advertising. Metro worked with a number of advertisers, commissioning focus groups to explore their brand values and look at how objectives could be achieved.

Metro went online with the launch of a promotions web site: www.metro.co.uk , built to harness the phenomenal response that Metro promotions deliver. It is the first online response mechanic launched by a media owner. 'We currently use this response mechanic for data collection, which is used both for customer profiling to further hone our distribution channels and for a variety of commercial applications,' says Wall.

Metwines (www.metwines.co.uk) was launched in November 2000, as a joint venture with Virgin Wines, offering a brand extension into the online wine business. Research shows that Metro readers, as urbanites, purchase a high volume of wine. Virgin Wines deliver the back-end fulfilment, but the experience is fully branded as Metwines.

Success story

As a new launch with a high cost base, Metro (London) was not projected to move into profitability until late 2000. It went into the black just 11 months from launch, well ahead of expectations. This success story is being repeated nationally, with the newspaper on track to move into profitability well ahead of original projections.

Metro reaches commuters in the North West, Midlands, Scotland, Yorkshire and the North East. Almost 800,000 copies are distributed each weekday. It is currently exploring other commercially viable opportunities to move the brand into new markets. There are also plans to expand the format both nationally into other urbanite cities, and internationally into key commuting conurbations across the world.

Source: *Marketing Business,* April 2001.

Questions

1. Metro used marketing research to inform various stages of its' marketing plan. From the Case Study identify three reasons why research was used.

2. Explain how each of the three types of research identified in 1. (above) might be collected.

3. The Case Study mentions the fact that Metro is exploring opportunities to move into new markets. Explain two important sources of data that Metro might use for this purpose, justifying your answer.

SUMMARY OF KEY POINTS

In this Session we have considered information's role in marketing, and covered the following key points:

- Marketing-oriented organisations are outward looking, keeping track of and responding to changes in the environment and in customer needs.

- The marketing planning process uses information to answer questions at each stage.

- In today's knowledge revolution, organisations are recognising the importance of knowledge management.

Improving and developing own learning

The following projects are designed to help you develop your knowledge and skills further by carrying out some research yourself. Feedback is not provided for this type of learning because there are no "answers" to be found, but you may wish to discuss your findings with colleagues and fellow students.

Project A

Talk to colleagues in your Marketing Department about information that is sourced on a regular basis. How is it obtained and stored?

Project B

Find out what the last piece of formal research commissioned by your Marketing Department was. What part of the planning process did it impact upon?

Project C

Visit your local commercial library or search the Internet to identify research reports that have been carried out for your industry. Look at the key sections of some of these reports. What aspects of the planning process could these inform?

Feedback to activities

Activity 1.1

Answers to this activity will vary depending on the organisation and industry you chose. However, the answer should include primary and secondary sources of information of an internal and external nature. Primary data is collected in order to achieve specific research objectives, whereas secondary data already exists and has been collected for a previous research project or for another purpose.

Activity 1.2

All the following types of media hold valuable information that enables organisations to take an informed and objective look at their past and current success and failures, so that they can learn from the information and make new plans for the future.

- Reports and business plans.
- Web links.
- Magazine articles.
- Conference notes.
- Sales reports.
- Email.
- Primary and secondary research.
- Books.

The type of information lost is more likely to be the disorganised/word of mouth type than the losing of books or reports.

There is a wealth of information that is commonly available in organisations that is not captured or organised in a formal manner for easy retrieval. Examples include helpline or customer service calls, sales reports, or even financial statistics. Individuals may know of useful web site addresses, but these may not be recorded centrally or shared. Likewise, those who attend conferences may collect useful documents, but these might not be circulated around the organisation.

Session 2

Marketing Information Systems

Introduction

This Session continues the section on information for marketing and looks at the Marketing Information System (MkIS). It also considers how organisations specify and filter valuable information from the large volumes of information available to them.

LEARNING OUTCOMES

At the end of this Session you will be able to:

■ Explain how organisations determine their marketing information requirements.

■ Identify and explain the key elements of user specifications for information.

■ Demonstrate an understanding of marketing management support systems and their different formats and components.

Marketing Information Systems (MkIS)

Sound marketing decisions rely on the availability of marketing information. The information can be drawn from sources internal or external to the organisation. The information might be used to develop strategy, to decide tactics, or to measure performance.

The use of objective, unbiased information, can assist marketing decision makers avoid assumptions and misunderstandings that would otherwise result in a poor marketing performance.

As an example of the importance of having unbiased and valid information consider the following aspects of marketing planning. Each aspect requires marketing information to facilitate the future planning of activities:

■ Decisions relating to marketing mix.

■ Product development.

■ Market segmentation profiling.

■ Evaluation of competitor strategies.

- Assessment of advertising effectiveness.

- Management of the marketing function.

- Development of customer service strategies.

Organisations may design software systems that collect data from the input data so that the financial forecasts generated are more accurate. For example, information about the usage of various products and/or buying behaviour could be assessed through statistics collected on distribution performance. Changes in environmental factors can be monitored to help contribute to the organisation's knowledge, aiding contingency planning. Imagine that the local supermarket was inaccessible by road for five days whilst new tarmac was laid. How much would this cost in lost sales? How could they make up lost sales through marketing efforts? Does there need to be a customer service strategy for the closure of the car park?

In order to develop an effective marketing information system the first step must be to identify the key decision makers requiring information, and to define the main applications for the information. Following this, the existing and potential sources of such information can then be identified (whether internal or external) and some decisions made regarding the storage and retrieval of future information. The information might then be classified into categories such as by product, by company, by customer/competitor, economic data, statistical data, technical information, etc., according to the specific needs of the organisation.

Marketing information should also be split into ongoing requirements (such as a press cutting service) and project based needs (where specific information is needed at a certain time). For instance, when launching a new product there will be a need to research consumer buying habits and to establish potential sales. Some new product launches have failed solely because they did not have enough stock to satisfy demand.

Figure 2.1: Marketing Information System

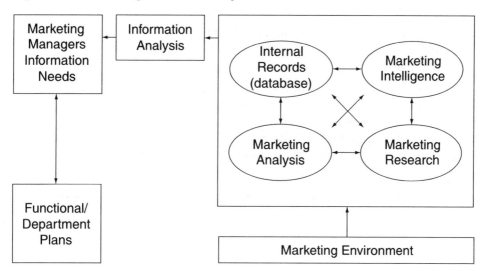

Filtering and determining information requirements

Organisations do not always make effective use of the information they hold. A systematic evaluation of the need for information is a prerequisite to avoiding the haphazard accumulation of underutilised or unused data.

Specific projects that require information may be split into a variety of different categories:

- **Descriptive studies** look at a number of variables within a situation (such as how many customers purchased Red Label tea last month), and may require statistical information to be collected from a survey.

- **Exploratory studies** look at a general area of enquiry and may reveal new insights into a subject.

- **Causal studies** look at causal relationships, such as if it is hot in October the likelihood is that 30% more ice cream will be bought than last year when October was cold.

Exploratory studies can be open-ended and difficult to manage because there is always more to learn. Using this approach requires discipline, a clear set of objectives and a framework within which to work. It also has the disadvantage of potentially bringing biased decisions into the equation. Descriptive and causal studies are more formal and are more likely to be conclusive.

The methodology chosen for collecting the required data will also depend on the way the decision-makers want the information to be presented and the method of interpretation to be used. This is important because if the data is presented in a raw format no conclusions can be drawn, so at least some interpretation must be carried out before it can be used for planning.

Primary and secondary data may be used depending on the urgency or the budget. Primary research is costly and time consuming, so secondary research is often used where there are strict time and budgetary constraints.

Activity 2.2

Prepare a presentation about the advantages and disadvantages of collecting marketing information in the three approaches described above.

Marketing management support systems

Management decision-making support systems are made up of internal and external data sources. The Marketing Information System (MkIS) is described by David Jobber as being:

'A system in which marketing information is formally gathered, stored and analysed and distributed to managers in accord with their informational needs on a regular and planned basis.'

Organisations collect, discuss, read and circulate all kinds of data and information. The challenge is to organise the inflow and outflow of information in such a way that enables meaningful conclusions to be drawn in a timely and efficient manner.

A manager's desk is bombarded daily by stock statistics, sales revenues, profit predictions, news articles, meeting minutes, business plans and research reports. How can they make sense of all this data? Financial information may have been collected for one purpose, but marketing may want it for another. Organisations that can deliver the right information, to the right person, at the right time, efficiently and effectively, have a source of potential competitive advantage.

Collecting and processing information is expensive. Therefore organisations and individuals need to consider such issues as:

- What information is essential/nice to have/inessential to collect? What would happen if we don't have it?

- What are the options for ensuring timely collection in a useful format?

- What are the costs and organisational value associated with each option? Over different timescales?

A strategic policy towards the collection and dissemination of data is required. The marketing department should analyse what information they require and what support and reporting systems need to be set up to satisfy their needs.

Internal and external information is fed into the MkIS. Some of this information will be collected in an ad hoc way through scanning the external environment, whilst other information is gathered from secondary sources such as market reports. All this information can then be entered into a computer database that collects data and organises it into a logical structure, so marketers are then able to search the system for relevant data.

For example, let's say a supermarket wants to gauge society's views on organic produce. The system would need to contain copies of press cuttings, articles from the press, TV programmes, national and local news, pressure group activity, competitor activity, and farming practices and subsidies. In this way a "body" of knowledge could be built up to support decision making.

Case Study

Remak International Plc

Remak International plc is a conglomerate with three divisions: homeware/ manufactured goods, trading and financial services. You have recently been appointed to the Financial Services Division as a Marketing Manager, with responsibility for identifying and developing new products. Within this remit your predecessor recently commissioned a marketing research report to examine the viability of a new investment fund to be offered initially in three major cities where your company operates, prior to a full launch of the product. You have some concerns with the way in which the original research was conducted through focus groups in only two of the three city locations. Furthermore, the six focus groups in each location were conducted with family members selected initially from a sample of students studying for their MBA at the business school of the university in each location. Initial results from this market research indicated that there would be a high demand for the product in each location for the Global Market Fund (GMF). The fund offers investors a choice of major quoted company shares from the world's top 200 companies. The average investor is expected to place US$10,000 in the fund. Annual projections forecast the fund to produce an annual return of 15% gross over the first five-year period of operation. The marketing research company that conducted the initial research forecast that the fund would attract 24,000 investors in each of the three city locations, more or less in equal proportions. Remak's GMF costs are:

Initial Marketing Research Report	US$10,000
Promotional Literature	US$36,000
Web Pages and Development (annual)	US$10,000
Administration Annual Charge 2% of the total fund	

Source: Management Information for Marketing Decisions exam paper, June 2001.

Questions

1. Identify the competitor information that you would want to gather for analysis before making your decision about the new product.

2. Identify sources of internal data that might be useful before making a decision.

3. List the concerns that you have about the research commissioned by your predecessor.

SUMMARY OF KEY POINTS

In this Session we have continued to consider the information needed in marketing and covered the following key points:

- The Marketing Information System (MkIS) provides a useful way of storing information and making sense of it.

- Information is available in vast quantities and managers need to be able to select what is useful and what is not.

- Database systems are not just useful in storing and analysing customer information, but can play a part in helping to provide a structure, whereby the information can be organised to meet marketing information needs.

Improving and developing own learning

The following projects are designed to help you develop your knowledge and skills further, by carrying out some research yourself. Feedback is not provided for this type of learning because there are no "answers" to be found, but you may wish to discuss your findings with colleagues and fellow students.

Project A

Draw a diagram, such as a flow chart, to show how you collect information from your customers and highlight the channels used for collecting data, storage and decision-making processes.

Project B

Talk to colleagues in your Marketing Department and find out whether your organisation has a formal MkIS. How is information filtered and stored? What suggestions for improvements can you make?

Project C

List all the information you have on your desk, including your email system. Identify:

■ Where did it come from?

■ How useful is it to your marketing role?

■ Did you request it or did it arrive unsolicited?

■ Might it be of use to a colleague?

■ If it is of no use to you, how might you stop it arriving in the future?

Feedback to activities

Activity 2.1

The external information will differ depending on the organisation and industry you chose. However, PEST factors are relevant to most organisations. It stands for:

Political
Economic
Social
Technological

Additional ongoing external information includes legal competitor information and customer attitudes, requirements and perceptions.

Activity 2.2

The three approaches can be briefly summarised as follows:

Descriptive	Exploratory	Causal
Requires clearly defined objectives. Structured framework. Primary research.	Open-ended research. Flexible. Informal. Tentative.	Confirms opinions. Conclusive. Could be large.

In your presentation you would identify examples of each, stating why the particular approach was used.

Session 3

Customer Relationship Management

Introduction

This Session deals specifically with customer information and the increasing importance of Customer Relationship Management (CRM). It considers the role of the database in managing customer information, in facilitating the personalisation of marketing communications, and in assessing the profitability of different customer groups.

LEARNING OUTCOMES

At the end of this Session you will be able to:

- Demonstrate an understanding of the application and benefits of customer databases.

- Explain the role of the database in Customer Relationship Management (CRM).

- Describe the process for setting up a database.

The customer database

'The old cardex system acted as our original database and we have developed sophisticated software programmes to take its place, so that we can use the information more efficiently and effectively. No longer do we have to search through our drawer for those business cards with notes on the back!'

Or do we? We should bear in mind the saying "garbage in, garbage out". No database system can overcome the problems caused by inputting inaccurate data or data that is not relevant. In contrast, an efficient database system will help us record current and historical data, giving us all the key facts we require to run an efficient, personalised, marketing system.

For example, a company may record all the details of every telephone and personal contact with a client, their contact details, their personal likes and dislikes, their past orders and future interests. This is valuable information that can be used by many departments for a variety of different uses. Perhaps the Accounts Department wants to check their credit worthiness. The Production Department might want to track back quotes and delivery promises. Marketing may want to send a mailshot informing all customers in the north-east about a forthcoming event.

The database should be designed with all these internal customers in mind. Many companies have either bought "off the shelf" database packages or not properly considered what their needs are when setting up their customer databases. The result is often an expensive database that is both inflexible and unable to provide sufficiently detailed information for the organisation to target specific groups for promotional purposes.

So, it is not just the recording of the data that is important. Data has to be manipulated and interpreted for different uses, and a well-designed database will serve the needs of a cross-functional team.

Customer databases are used to improve relationships with customers and to ensure that a continuous, meaningful dialogue is part of the customer relationship management process. Sophisticated databases enable organisations to identify individual buying patterns and thereby send personally targeted promotions. To be greeted by name is a most impressive form of recognition, and all the while the database can collect valuable information that will help marketers profile customer segments more accurately, so that their products and communications can be tailored more effectively.

The database needs to be designed so that it can support various marketing activities and decision making. This may mean that data needs to be imported and exported to other software programmes, so that meaningful reports and interpretations can be made from the raw data.

Databases can support the following marketing activities:

- Direct marketing – as discussed above.

- Product development – relevant searches might identify trends in consumer buying patterns that can be followed up by additional research. Alternatively, the information collated from the search may support research findings.

- Customer Relationship Management (CRM) – by facilitating appropriate communications, such as specifically targeted promotions.

- Profiling segments – identifying small or specific groups with common characteristics.

- Customer research – relevant searches can reveal changes in customer buying behaviour for example.

- Sales prospecting – enabling cross or up-selling.

Activity 3.1

Looking at your own database system, draw a flow chart of how information is collected from the customer and how it is used for various aspects of internal decision making. Are there any improvements that could be made to streamline the system and make it more user-friendly?

Customer Relationship Marketing (CRM)

Database-driven direct marketing can be an efficient and economic way to find new customers, develop additional business with existing customers, and build customer loyalty. "Relationship" marketing, as it is often called, initially involves the building of a simple but customised relational database. A relational database enables sophisticated and complex searches to be made because different databases "relate to each other", so data from each is used in a single search.

Database marketing depends on the collection of accurate data about existing and potential customers. Online access to client databases, using secure access systems, enables the management of reward redemptions, immediate responses to customer service queries, and keeping customers aware of latest developments.

The main applications of database marketing are:

- Direct mail.
- Loyalty marketing.
- Telemarketing.
- Distributor management.
- Campaign planning.

Database marketing is targeted at those customers most likely to respond; those who have had previous contact with the company or who fit the profile of a typical purchaser.

The database needs to incorporate sophisticated search facilities so that criteria can be used to "segment" various target groups. Typical information held might include:

Consumer Marketing	Business to Business
Address and telephone number.	Name and address.
Fax and email address.	Size of company.
Product queries.	Contact details.
Past sales.	DMU (Decision-Making Unit).
Lifestyle information.	Discounts and allowances.
Age and income.	Past sales history.

More and more companies are adopting a telemarketing strategy as the spearhead of their marketing initiatives, so accurate databases are playing an increasingly crucial role in marketing development.

The following Case Studies (from www.dbsdata.co.uk) illustrate how CRM can be applied.

Major European Mobile Phone Distributor

Europe's leading distributor of mobile phones, responding to intense competition, engaged a consultancy company to contact retailers and other potential outlets for mobile pre-pay telephones, to educate the marketplace, and where appropriate, offer the opportunity to stock and sell pre-paid telephones in anticipation of the Christmas boom.

Having sorted and cleaned their database, the agency made more than 30,000 contacts and successfully increased the organisation's market share, contributing significantly to their bottom line.

International Biotechnology Company

Having acquired a new subsidiary supplying cloned genetic markers to the burgeoning biological research industry, a long-established biotechnology company needed a new approach that would allow them to identify and quantify the interest levels for various biological products.

Working very closely with their highly experienced sales team, the database was cleaned, and through newly identified research activities, numerous appointments for professional sales representatives to make face-to-face presentations to the leading researchers in some of the country's biggest pharmaceutical and biological research organisations were made.

The success of this campaign lead to two other projects that helped revive and invigorate other aspects of their overall marketing efforts.

You may also like to visit www.dmconcepts.co.uk for additional examples and information.

Setting up the database

To conduct database-driven direct marketing successfully, organisations need to create a database and manage it so that customer details are up to date. There is nothing worse than sending a mailshot only to find half of the recipients are no longer in the job or worse still dead!

Online companies such as Yell Data offer customised mailing lists of business contacts to use for targeted direct mail and telemarketing campaigns.

However, organisations can create their own business lists to target prospects just by collecting information. Below are some of the methods that may be used to collect information about customers:

- Seminar and exhibition attendees.
- Market research.
- Promotions.
- Application forms.
- Complaints.
- Enquiries.
- Warranty and guarantee cards.
- Sales force records.
- Response to previous direct marketing.

- Offering samples in exchange for name and address.

- Exchanging data with other companies.

The database can be sourced from in-house records, through a market research agency, by co-operating with other brands that have similar customer profiles, or through the continual collection of information from enquiries and telephone calls.

The database will need to be managed by using database enhancement software to search for duplicate records and clean the list, check contact details, and enhance the contact record with additional information, such as email and web site addresses.

Activity 3.2

Identify three reasons why databases must be "cleaned" and duplications removed regularly.

Case Study

The customer's champion

Dr. Martha Rogers is on a mission. Her goal? To convert any of those unreconstructed marketers out there who continue to follow the old rules of mass marketing. Her credo, and one to which she has been loyal for the best part of a decade, is that customer centricity is the only way to go.

Customer centricity is another name for one-to-one, a term she and her partner in the Peppers & Rogers group, Don Peppers, first gave life to with the publication of their seminal book in 1993, 'The One-to-One Future'. She now prefers talking about customer-focused strategy but, whatever you call it, the message is the same: you can't have a business without customers. This isn't about just acquiring them however. Even more importantly you have to keep and grow them.

This turns the traditional approaches to marketing upside down she believes. In fact, she goes further: 'I don't really think about marketing so much any more, except with the word "mass" in front of it,' she says dismissively. 'To me, marketing is mass marketing. All the rest of what we are talking about is something bigger. It is something that has a higher, more enterprise-wide connotation.'

'It is about critical strategy. When we first started, Don and I coined the phrase "one-to-one marketing". But we don't even use that any more because it suggests that one-to-one relationships can be built out of the marketing department. And that just can't happen.'

To Rogers, the marketing department as it is currently constituted is focused on getting customers. Relationships, on the other hand, although there is obviously an element of acquisition, are mostly about keeping and growing customers. And that's something the marketing department can't possibly do on its own.

Customer relationships are the hub

'It takes all of us in an organisation. Traditional marketing is a spoke of the wheel. But customer relationships are the hub. And that means everyone has to ask: how does our collective obligation to build stronger relationships and create more valuable customers change my role from what it used to be in a product-centred world to what is becoming an information-rich world? Every decision I take during the day has to go through that filter. And the answer to that question will be different in different parts of the organisation.'

The golden rule, Rogers says, is to treat customers' as you would like to be treated. But how do you do that if customers number in the thousands or even millions? What makes this increasingly viable are the modern technological tools that not only enable companies to find their most valuable customers, but to tailor the relationships according to customers' requirements.

The problem, she says, is that too often those at the top who should be driving this transformation don't have it on what she calls their "radar screen" because they are not rewarded for stewardship of their most valuable customers, they are only rewarded for short-term results.

So they delegate this "customer relationship stuff" to the marketing team, which has grown up in the world of marketing as branding, advertising and/or sales promotion. 'Its no wonder marketing people are scratching their heads.'

It's one of the reasons she spends so much time on the road talking about her vision of how companies need to change to stay in business. She was in the UK in September for example, to run a master class on customer centricity at the UK Marketing Forum, hammering home her belief that being customer-smart and customer-centric is simply common business sense.

Mass marketing's diminishing returns

'With mass marketing,' she argues, 'you face diminishing returns over time because once you reach a certain level of customers, it becomes more expensive to win those at the margin if you want to boost market share. In the one-to-one age, on the other hand, customer relationships themselves become the source of competitive differentiation and hence value.'

After all, if a company invests in building a learning relationship with customers, it's in the customers' own interests to stay loyal because they have also invested in the relationship. It brings down costs as well, since not only does this lessen the customer acquisition budget, but the cost of serving a loyal customer is lower.

This isn't about "firing" customers she stresses. You have to tread very carefully and make sure that when you begin to segment customers according to their worth, that you don't treat anyone badly, because bad PR will never engender trust. But if they do leave, don't cry.

Internalising CRM

The problem for companies is finding the right sort of person with the right talents and skills who not only understands this but, even more importantly, is able to push the necessary changes throughout the organisation. The good ones, she says, are those who truly understand and internalise "real" customer relationship management (CRM). They don't embark on a CRM programme simply to do what she calls "better targeted harassment" or to make the call centre more efficient.

'CRM is such a misused term. It's too much about what's in it for us, not for both sides. What you need are people who can think about one to one both strategically and tactically. They are willing to break the rules. They are the people who, if you prick their finger, they bleed one to one.'

In the US for instance, Rogers is seeing the emergence of a new type of person called a "chief relationship officer" to fill this role.

Building up a reputation for helping clients understand what they have to do in regard to their customers has helped the Peppers & Rogers group grow to the point where there are now 220 employees in offices around the world. But this wouldn't have happened without that fateful meeting 12 years ago when Martha met Don.

It was 1990. She was in academia, teaching marketing at a university in Ohio, having acquired a doctorate in marketing/communications along the way in what had begun as a career in advertising and progressed through to being a professor. He worked in advertising on Madison Avenue in New York. One day she took some of her students to a talk Don Peppers was giving at the local advertising club.

As she recalls, 'Here was this speaker talking about something that I had been trying to discuss with my colleagues in the department. And that was: didn't we need to rethink mass media and mass marketing in the face of a proliferation of media? I thought that, surely, because of that, we can't keep doing things in the same way. And that was before we had the Internet.'

Rogers went up to Don Peppers afterwards, introduced herself and said, please, couldn't he write a book about this because there was such a desperate need for one? Within a matter of minutes they had agreed to do one together. Thus began both a stream of co-authored books selling well over a million copies, but also an enduring partnership that has thrived despite her living in Ohio with her family and Peppers based halfway across the country at the head office in Connecticut.

The arrival of the Internet, of course, has given fresh impetus to the need to treat customers as individuals. The Internet presents both a range of opportunities but also challenges for companies trying to get closer to customers she believes.

For example, how much personalisation is feasible? How much is essential? How can incoming messages and interactivity be handled in the same way across the organisation? And then there is the privacy issue. The promise of privacy when it comes to customer information is becoming an integral element in building successful customer relationships. This is not only because various governments are taking a far greater interest in privacy protection, but also because customer information is becoming a company's most vital asset. It's also a growing part of the consultancy's work. Because if you lose trust and fail to be seen as a trusted agent, Rogers believes you lose any competitive advantage customer information brings. Think about privacy, she urges, as something you do for your customers.

Although both she and Don Peppers oversee client projects at a high level, Rogers herself is far more involved in flying around the world talking about the issues involved in implementing a customer-focused strategy. She feels passionately about getting companies to see the light: 'I think that a lot of them are getting it wrong and I really believe that if we were to do all this stuff right it would help save the economy.'

When it comes to marketers in particular, she reckons they are going through some sort of identification crisis because they know there is something to this idea of relationship building but aren't quite sure what to do about it. So, does she have any advice for today's marketers, apart from unlearning the old ideas about mass marketing?

'Perhaps a good place to start is to define what information you need, and how you are going to get it. And make sure that any efforts you make don't wait till the end pay off. Look for quick wins. And then let the results speak for themselves.'

Source: *Marketing Business,* November/December 2002.

Questions

1. Explain the term "customer centricity" as it is used in the Case Study.

2. The Case Study stresses that CRM should benefit both parties in the relationship. Identify three benefits that CRM might offer customers.

3. The Case Study talks about protecting the privacy of customers. Identify any legislation in your country that exists to protect this privacy.

SUMMARY OF KEY POINTS

In this Session we have introduced the concept of Customer Relationship Management (CRM) and covered the following key points:

- Technology has enabled the development of the database into a powerful tool for the management of customer information.

- A customer database can be used for many purposes, including:

  - Direct mail.

  - Loyalty marketing.

  - Telemarketing.

  - Distributor management.

  - Campaign planning.

- Information for setting up a database can initially be obtained from many sources, including:
  - Seminar and exhibition attendees.
  - Market research.
  - Promotions.
  - Application forms.
  - Complaints.
  - Enquiries.
  - Warranty and guarantee cards.
  - Sales force records.
  - Response to previous direct marketing.
  - Offering samples in exchange for name and address.
  - Exchanging data with other companies.
- It is essential that any database is kept up to date through regular "cleaning", or customer relationships can be damaged rather than enhanced.

Improving and developing own learning

The following projects are designed to help you develop your knowledge and skills further, by carrying out some research yourself. Feedback is not provided for this type of learning because there are no "answers" to be found, but you may wish to discuss your findings with colleagues and fellow students.

Project A

Reflect on occasions where you have been asked to provide your name and address and personal details. How many databases do you think you are listed with? In what circumstances have organisations' capitalised on having your name on their database? What are the implications for data protection?

Project B

Write a case study about how direct marketing has improved sales within your own organisation, explaining how the data on your customers was sourced and filtered for the database.

Project C

Talk to colleagues in your Marketing Department about what form of customer database is maintained. How is information obtained? How often is it cleaned and duplications removed? What purposes is it used for?

Feedback to activities

Activity 3.1

Each database system will differ, however, the main principles remain the same.

Figure 3.1: Collection of data

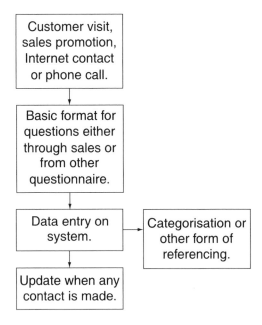

Information can be organised into various categories. This makes the database easily searchable, so it can be used for different activities. You may wish to analyse the customer base by:

- Geography.
- Yearly spend.
- Usage – seasonal averages.
- Interests and needs.
- Lifestyle.
- Product types.

Such information can then help you with customer profiling and sending mailshots. However, there may be many other uses for the information, and the depth of information you need to collect will be determined by your industry sector and the sophistication of your marketing research requirements.

Activity 3.2

There are many reasons why a database should be cleaned and duplications removed. These include:

- Avoiding upsetting customers through incorrectly spelling names.
- Appearing unprofessional by wasting money mailing more than once to the same customer.
- Avoiding upsetting families by mailing a deceased family member.
- Tarnishing the image of the organisation.
- Mailing confidential information to an incorrect address.

Session 4

More about data

Introduction

This Session continues to look at the ways in which data is stored and specifically at more sophisticated ways of manipulating data to profile customers and prospects. It explores the role of data warehouses, data marts and data mining in helping to gain customer insight. Finally, the differences between database marketing and marketing research are considered.

LEARNING OUTCOMES

At the end of this Session you will be able to:

- Explain how organisations profile customers and prospects.

- Explain the principles of data warehouses, data marts and data mining.

- Explain the relationship between database marketing and marketing research.

Profiling customers and prospects

The profiling of customers and prospects has already been touched upon in Session 2, under the section that described a marketing information system and discussed how the information might be used.

The next sections explore the principles of data warehousing and data mining, but first we should consider the types of information that are useful for marketing.

The main types of customer data are categorised by Alan Wilson as being:

- Behavioural, which as the name suggests, relates to customer behaviour with regard to all aspects of buying. The many sources of this type of data include customer complaints, enquiries, payment processing and other paperwork. However, the database only holds information about **what** customers do, not **why** they demonstrate that behaviour.

- Profile, which can be sources from profiling systems such as ACORN and CACI (see glossary) and lifestyle databases. Company databases also provide standard data and information on organisations for business-to-business markets.

- Volunteered data, provided by the customer when completing questionnaires, at the point of purchase, or when expressing an interest in a product or service.

- Attributed data, which can be extracted from marketing research results, and is general in nature to protect confidentiality. It highlights possibilities such as teenagers are more likely to own a specific type of mobile phone or be interested in playing games on their mobile.

Activity 4.1

Taking the organisation you work for or one you know well, assess the information needs the Marketing Department might have for launching a new product/service into a new market in the UK.

Data storage

As discussed in the previous Session, a database is essentially a structured collection of data. In a business context, a database usually relates to a particular subject or has a specific purpose, such as the storage of customer information.

Contrary to popular belief, a database need not be stored on a computer. However, in reality most modern databases are computer-based because of the speed and convenience with which these systems can handle, manage and present data.

The increased use of computer networks and corporate Intranets means that data stored in databases can now be shared and accessed by nominated users both quickly and cheaply.

Data warehousing

A data warehouse is a large database that uses considerable amounts of stored transactional data to analyse a range of business activities and functions. The results of this analysis can be used to support decision making.

For example, an organisation can use a data warehouse to:

- Assist with market segmentation.

- Identify latent customer needs.

- Make distribution decisions.

- Provide an indication of the production levels required.

For more details about data warehousing see the article "What is Data Warehousing?" by Dan Lazar at http://www.marketingprofs.com/Perspect/datawarehousing.asp.

Data mining

Data mining is the term given to the complex sifting of existing data to identify patterns and establish relationships. Data mining selects, explores, and models large amounts of data to uncover previously unknown relationships and patterns.

When data mining, marketers often look for the following parameters:

- **Association** – a pattern where one event is connected to another.

- **Sequence or path analysis** – a pattern where one event leads to another, later event.

- **Classification** – the emergence of new patterns.

- **Clustering** – finding and documenting newly discovered groups of facts.

- **Forecasting** – discovering patterns in data to predict the future.

Data mining techniques are used in mathematics, cybernetics and genetics. A relatively new term, "web mining", is used to describe the type of data mining used in Internet-based Customer Relationship Management (CRM) systems. This technique takes advantage of the information gathered via a web site to look for patterns in visitor behaviour.

Let's look at an example of data mining in the video rental market. Blockbuster Video (http://www.blockbuster.com or http://www.blockbuster.co.uk) is a leader in the business of renting films on video.

Blockbuster uses a number of systems, including a CRM system. Data is extracted (mined) from customer databases for marketing research purposes, and consumers are asked to indicate the types of film they prefer to watch.

Based on the preferences they express, personalised automated calls are then made to the customers (or emails sent), offering them the option to reserve a film that matches their individual preferences.

Data marts

Data marts are department or subject specific databases that put the right information into the hands of decision makers as they need it. They rely on a data warehouse or main database, and contain information that has been extracted and transformed so that it can be easily analysed and accessed.

They speed up the decision-making process because, having extracted relevant data, the "queries" made on the data are only made on the relevant data, not on all of the data in the warehouse.

Storage media

The electronic data collected from various research activities must be stored in some way for later use. A storage medium is the method used to record the data. Examples of these include:

- **Computer diskettes** – a general storage medium (such as the common 3.5" floppy disk), used to store electronic files and documents, but limited in storage capacity.

- **CD-ROMs** – one of the most popular formats for storing relatively large amounts of electronic information, including digital sound and video. Typically, a CD-ROM can store around 400 times as much information as a standard floppy disk.

- **DVDs** – these disks provide even more data storage capacity than CD-ROMs, and are commonly used for playing full motion videos.

- **Smart cards** – these incorporate a microchip to store details about the user, including the cardholder's purchasing habits. Examples include loyalty cards and phone cards.

As the need for more data grows, and the capacity and speed of computers increases, so new storage media are continually being developed to meet the needs of users.

Activity 4.2

There are various media available for storing electronic data, including those listed below.

- Computer 3.5" diskettes.

- CD-ROMs.

- DVDs.

- Smart cards.

With marketing and marketing communications in mind, suggest some potential uses for each of the above storage media.

Research and databases

Informed marketing decision making is essential for achieving a marketing orientation. Information is obtained by both formal and informal means. For example, exhibitions can be a major source of information from customers, suppliers and key opinion formers. If this informally gathered information is not captured in one place, accessible to all, then the "knowledge" is lost. Many organisations therefore include the capture of information as part of their staff debriefing following events such as exhibitions.

Organisations also collect **internal** and **external** data. For example, internal data may be monitored to assess sales trends and to take decisions on sales efforts and marketing priorities. If sales are falling or there is likely to be a seasonal low, then activities can be put in place to boost sales. External data, such as economic or social trends, also need to be captured, and customer information may well help indicate new attitudes or assist in improving product development projects.

Marketing research can be **ad-hoc, continuous** or **project based.** Research data is also either primary (collected on a project basis, specifically for a given objective), or secondary (coming to the researcher second hand, with other people having compiled the data for a different set of objectives).

Often secondary research informs the specification for primary research, and information already held on an existing database can be very helpful in the planning stages of any major project.

Information from the database that could be utilised includes:

- Names and addresses of research participants.

- Customer profiles.

- Customer by product type.

- Contact profiles and Decision-Making Unit (DMU) information.

The database can also support the sampling process. For example, if random sampling is used then it is easy to draw random names from the database. Focus groups can be sought using specific criteria such as geographical area etc.

Research plays a major role within the marketing audit in reviewing previous marketing activities and looking at new trends that may provide product and market development opportunities. Market research is also used to assess customer satisfaction and perceptions of the brand. However, care must be taken to act in an ethical manner, so ensure that any information gained when conducting marketing research is only used for the purpose stated. Customers' permission should be requested if information is to be entered into a database that will be used for other purposes in the future, such as in a sales campaign. The best way of dealing with this is to make sure that the data is anonymous before it is analysed.

A customer database gives an organisation the potential for regular communication with their current and potential client base. A well-designed and well-managed database is a useful tool for developing targeted customer communications. When selling a company, the customer database and the information stored on those customers, is often regarded as a valuable part of the company valuation.

Activity 4.3

Prepare a presentation to your Manager explaining the likely uses for the information you have stored on your database.

Case Study

Data, data everywhere

A good, clean, well-maintained customer database is arguably any company's best asset. The trouble is for many companies it can often seem like an impossible dream. Not only does customer data reside in different areas of the business but, in addition, in the day-to-day grind of running the business no one has the time to keep the data up-to-date, let alone gather it all in one place.

The fact is, however, that this ideal of the clean, well-maintained customer database is simply too valuable to ignore. Once in place, it opens up a wealth of possibilities for the marketing team, enabling them to segment customers according to the types of products they are interested in, the time of year they are likely to buy, their age, demographic profile or past purchasing history. In the b2b arena, it can help companies target the right sort of businesses in the hunt for new customers. The sales force can be organised and managed more effectively. The benefits then are obvious. What's not so obvious is how this ideal is achieved.

Gary Selby, Joint Managing Director of the database consultants Information Arts, splits the database operation into two distinct sections. The back end involves compiling the database in the first instance, then secondly ensuring its integrity and quality from there on in. This, he admits, is easier said than done. 'It's a journey, never a destination, because by definition the day after you have compiled your database it starts deteriorating,' says Selby.

To counter this, modern database programs are configured to update themselves from data from the client's legacy systems on a daily, weekly or monthly basis, even hourly if there's so much data flowing into the client company that that is what's needed.

Selby says that the vast majority of Information Arts' clients ask his company to carry out the back-end maintenance for them. They can then concentrate on the revenue-earning front end; the software tools that help marketers profile their database and put together well-targeted marketing campaigns. The cost of this database maintenance can range he says from £1,000 to £30,000 per month for a blue-chip organisation, on top of the initial build cost of between £20,000 and £50,000.

In addition to simply updating records from the clients' own systems, this ongoing maintenance ensures that duplicate records are removed, checks for changes of address are made, and it also matches the company's database against the various preference services (telephone, post and fax) to ensure that companies who have asked not to be mailed, faxed or called are not.

'The data may be clean and accurate, but is it as detailed as it could be? By comparing the customer data a business holds against the total universe of potential customers, companies in the business-to-business arena can identify new prospects and identify those prospects with the greatest potential to do business with them,' says Steve Cook, Managing Director of the business-to-business database company, Market Location.

Typical data enhancements might include the names of senior executives at businesses on the company's database, the number of staff they employ, their turnover and their SIC (Standard Industrial Classification) code, which defines exactly what the company does. 'By SIC coding a company's existing database and overlaying other factors such as size and location, the company can build up a profile of its typical customer,' Cook says. They can then target prospects who come close to this profile and who should therefore have greater potential to become customers than companies targeted at random. 'You can build models of potential. You're doing business with this type of organisation. There are another 3,000 companies that meet those criteria. Your current penetration of the total universe of that type of company is x, so the potential is y,' Cook says.

Data visualisation

When it comes to analysing or querying the customer database in order to target sections of it and put marketing campaigns together, there is no shortage of data visualisation tools available to do the job. In years gone by many of these tools could only be accessed via the IT department, with the marketer's queries joining the queue along with those from the rest of the organisation. This situation still persists in a surprising number of companies.

'The problem with this is that by the time you get the results you've forgotten why you wanted them,' says John Regan, Managing Director of database and data analysis company Cognisance.

At the other extreme are software packages such as Viper from Smartfocus (www.smartfocus.com) and BusinessObjects from the company of the same name (www.businessobjects.com). These tools are relatively affordable (BusinessObjects starts from around £6,000) and enable marketers to raise queries from their desktop without having to rely on the IT department. The only drawback says Regan is that the data is pre-processed, rather than queried in real time, which means there is a limit to how often queries can be scheduled. The results are usually, at best, a week out of date.

This may be an acceptable compromise in many situations but it means that when a company wants to run a campaign it needs to get back to the real database to pull off the relevant, up-to-date names and addresses. It can fall down in situations where a quick response is needed.

'If you suddenly have a series of complaints all on one day, there's considerable value in being able to respond to these on the same day,' says Regan. 'If it's a week before you're able to see who has complained recently, and you see that they were all your best customers, you really would have liked that information five days before.'

The ideal solution of course is a sophisticated CRM (Customer Relationship Management) solution, which not only looks at the live database in real time, but can even be programmed to react automatically to given events, like complaints for example. The only drawback here is the cost, which often runs into several hundred thousands, if not millions, of pounds.

Another option is one of the more technical analysis solutions such as SAS (www.sas.com) or SPSS (www.spss.com), which allow a company to extract data from a database, produce highly technical analysis, and write information straight back to the database. 'The positive side of this is that you can really get into the nuts and bolts of the data and really understand in great detail what's going on, and it's easy to export the results into something like Excel to put a presentation together,' says Regan. 'The limitation is that the person using the software needs to be a qualified statistician who understands both the theory and the practice of the statistics they are looking at.' Regan's point here is that a statistician will naturally hone in on results that throw up interesting facts about a campaign. It's then down to a senior marketer to decide whether the result is relevant.

'Let's say 10% of respondents to a campaign are over 50, compared to only 5% of the customer database,' says Regan. 'The statistician will pick that up as an interesting result. But the marketer then needs to recognise that it's still only 10% of the respondents and ask, what about the other 90%?'

Market Location's Steve Cook makes a similar point. 'Senior marketers must get involved in the analysis... [it] is not always a very exciting task, but to leave it to junior staff is a mistake. You need the thought leadership to know which questions to ask of the database and to know what other questions the answers to those questions raise.'

Clearly, building and maintaining a live customer database is no easy task. However, can any business afford to ignore the tricky issues that real insight into its customers' behaviour will raise?

Source: *Marketing Business,* July/August, 2002.

Questions

1. The Case Study talks about splitting the database into "front-end" and "back-end" operations. Explain the difference between the two systems.

2. Explain what is meant by the term "customer insight".

3. The Case Study argues for the "completeness" of data (detail and relevancy), and mentions adding a "SIC" code for business-to-business marketing. How might this benefit the company using the database?

SUMMARY OF KEY POINTS

In this Session we have explored data further and covered the following key points:

- Customer databases provide information on purchase behaviour, customer loyalty and customer response.

- They only describe "what" and not "why".

- Types of customer data include:

  - Behavioural data.

  - Profile data.

  - Volunteered data.

  - Attributed data.

- A data warehouse is a large database storing transactional data and enabling insightful analysis.

- Data mining selects, explores, and models large amounts of data to uncover previously unknown relationships and patterns.

- Marketing research should be transparent about its usage and should not be used to "sell" to respondents.

Improving and developing own learning

The following projects are designed to help you develop your knowledge and skills further, by carrying out some research yourself. Feedback is not provided for this type of learning because there are no "answers" to be found, but you may wish to discuss your findings with colleagues and fellow students.

> **Project A**
>
> Talk to colleagues in your IT Department. What types of information are used regularly by your organisation and for what purposes?

> **Project B**
>
> Talk to colleagues in your Marketing Department. What types of information are held by your organisation and how do marketers use them? Compare your answers here with your findings for Project A. How do they differ?

> **Project C**
>
> Try to find an example of how databases have been used to profile customers in your organisation. How has this information been used since the analysis was undertaken?

Feedback to activities

Activity 4.1

The new product/service should have a number of benefits, so the aim is to establish a customer profile whose needs best fit the benefits offered. The first task is to research the buying habits and needs and wants of the target market. Once it's clear who the product is aimed at, then a picture can be built up of the leisure interests and business habits associated with this customer segment; where they buy, how they buy and how often. Media research will also be needed to establish how best to communicate with them.

This information will be essential for planning the marketing mix.

Activity 4.2

With marketing and marketing communications in mind, some potential uses of the media indicated might include:

Computer 3.5" diskettes

These disks have a limited storage capacity, but they could be used by marketing staff and management to back up personal files, or to transport files (such as Word documents or Spreadsheets) from one computer to another. For example, a spreadsheet containing details of sales records could be saved to a 3.5" disk, and the spreadsheet file could then be transferred to a laptop or notepad, so that the document could be viewed or developed, perhaps whilst the user is travelling on a train.

Today, businesses make relatively little use of floppy disks compared to a few years ago since machines can now be networked to transfer data.

CD-ROMs

As more electronic information can be stored on a CD-ROM, this medium is most likely to be used to store or disseminate large amounts of information, programs or sound and video. In practice, CD-ROMS are commonly used to circulate documents or computer programs that would be too large to fit on a 3.5" disk. CD-ROMS are also used in a marketing context to incorporate video, or even as a medium to circulate "stand-alone" copies of a corporate web site. Provided users have an Internet connection, they can open a link on the CD that will take them directly to the actual web site, for updates etc. Other possible uses of CD-ROMs include marketing training, promotions, and corporate communications (including the circulation of company annual reports).

DVDs

Although not yet frequently used for promotional purposes, the enormous capacity of DVDs suggests that these disks will be used in various marketing contexts in the future – especially in situations where there is a requirement for a considerable amount of full motion video. Many of the possible applications are similar to those covered in the CD-ROM section above.

Smart cards

As smart cards incorporate a microchip to store details about the user, including the cardholder's purchasing habits, they hold various advantages over many of the other storage media. Most visitors to a supermarket or other retail store will be familiar with the use of supermarket loyalty cards or store credit cards. Retailers can issue smart cards to regular shoppers and gain a personal and financial profile of each user. This can help retailers understand customer purchasing habits and preferences, and help them improve their market segmentation. It will also help them develop products and services that are really popular with customers. The data of course also has some value in itself, and provided permission has been given, this data can be sold as a commodity (since it is of value to other suppliers).

Activity 4.3

This is just an example of the sources and uses of information held on a typical marketing database. As you can see, the information on the database can be used for a wide range of market research activities.

Types of information and likely source	Product Development Research	Customer Satisfaction Surveys	Competitor Research	Market Trends	Marketing Promotions	Sales Prospecting Forecasting
Customer contact details		✓				
Sales order history				✓		✓
Customer complaints	✓					
Informal information about trends	✓			✓		
Competitor information			✓	✓		
Seasonal trends	✓					✓
Decision-Making Unit (DMU)					✓	
Personal interests					✓	✓
Lifestyle characteristics	✓				✓	

Session 5

Marketing research – the industry and the process

Introduction

This Session examines the structure of the marketing research industry and the role of the various players in the industry. It explores the different types of information providers working within the industry, and then moves on to examine the stages involved in the marketing research process.

LEARNING OUTCOMES

At the end of this Session you will be able to:

- Describe the nature and structure of the marketing research industry.

- Describe the roles of the various players in the marketing research industry.

- Explain the stages of the marketing research process.

The market research industry

The UK market research industry is reported to be worth almost £1billion. There has been a growing concentration in the industry, which has resulted in a polarisation between the super groups of global players offering co-ordinated worldwide research (with the ability to invest considerable sums in the development of technology), and smaller boutique or niche operators that specialise in particular types of research or specific business sectors.

Market research is sometimes considered to fall within a broader business information market. There are about 139 VAT registered companies offering market research services in the UK; from small partnerships to large multinationals. But with the large number of individual consultants in the industry, it is suggested that there may be as many as 400 companies in this sector in the UK.

It is widely believed that quantitative research accounts for some 80 per cent of industry revenue, with the remainder accounted for by qualitative research. Face-to-face interviews account for about half of the industry turnover, while telephone interviews account for about 20 per cent and postal surveys 8 per cent. The remaining 22 per cent is accounted for by other methods such as observation and Internet surveys.

British Market Research Association (BMRA)

The BMRA (www.bmra.org.uk) is the main association body representing all the main market research companies in the UK (apart from AC Nielsen).

It was formed in April 1998 by the merger of two established trade associations, ABMRC (Association of British Market Research Companies) and AMSO (Association of Market Research Survey Organisations).

The main aims of the Association are to increase professionalism and promote confidence in the market research industry, both in the UK and internationally, as well as represent the professional and commercial interests of its' member companies.

BMRA is the single trade association for the market research industry and now has approximately 200 members, representing in total around £820 million of turnover, an estimated 80% of the UK market research industry.

The BMRA Selectline service offers assistance in locating a market research agency. This allows the user to specify by market sector, by research methodology, by research expertise and by geographical coverage. It also allows them to specify fieldwork only, fieldwork and Data Processing (DP), or DP only.

The Market Research Society (MRS)

The Market Research Society (www.mrs.org.uk) is the professional association representing individuals in the market research industry, but typically has membership in most market research companies. It has its own Code of Conduct to which members must adhere, and publishes an annual handbook (the MRS Yearbook), which is a valuable source of information on MRS members and most UK market research companies. With over 8,000 members in more than 50 countries, the Market Research Society claims to be the world's largest international membership organisation for professional researchers and others engaged or interested in market, social or opinion research.

The Society runs a range of training courses and has its own nationally recognised Diploma – the MRS Diploma.

The European Society for Opinion and Marketing Research (ESOMAR)

Somewhat confusingly ESOMAR is the World Association of Opinion and Marketing Research Professionals (www.esomar.org). Their web site gives the following details.

'European by origin, global by nature, ESOMAR was founded in 1948 as the European Society for Opinion and Marketing Research, and unites over 4,000 members in 100 countries; both users and providers of research.

Members come from all industry sectors; from advertising and media agencies, universities and business schools, as well as public institutions and government authorities.

Membership in ESOMAR is open to all those who are actively involved in, or concerned with, professional standards in opinion and marketing research.

All ESOMAR members, as well as the management of the companies listed in the ESOMAR directory, undertake to comply with the ICC/ESOMAR International Code of Marketing and Social Research Practice. The Code has been jointly drafted by ESOMAR and the International Chamber of Commerce (ICC), and is endorsed by the major national professional bodies around the world.

ESOMAR has an extensive series of conferences, seminars and publications, designed to improve professional knowledge and skills. Research World is its' monthly publication and the ESOMAR Directory (published annually) provides information on members and research companies.'

Activity 5.1

Marketing research can be expensive, and one way to reduce the cost is to take part in an omnibus survey. Omnibus research uses a collaborative approach, whereby a number of clients buy space on a survey form either as a "one-off" or on a regular basis.

Go to the BMRA web site and locate the names of some agencies that can offer general national omnibus services.

Check the Code of Conduct of the Market Research Society (www.mrs.org.uk) and find out what the guidelines are regarding confidentiality of respondents to a survey.

Selecting a research agency

The choice of agency can depend on a number of criteria, including their:

- Track record (if you've used them before).
- Experience in your sector.
- Location.
- Client list.
- Testimonials from other clients.
- Experience of the market/region.
- Size/resources.
- Creativity.
- Approach.
- Understanding of the subject.
- "Chemistry" with you.

One of the key distinctions between the various players is their different skill sets and areas of specialisation.

One can distinguish firstly between those agencies offering mainly qualitative research and those offering quantitative studies.

Some agencies may specialise in particular techniques, such as in-depth, face to face, telephone, focus groups or omnibus research.

Some agencies specialise in business-to-business research, whilst others may undertake mainly consumer research. Some agencies specialise by age group, perhaps with particular expertise in research with children, or specialise by sector, such as:

Food and drink.
Public sector/local government.
Automotive industry.
Financial research.
Trade/retail research.
Media research.

Other specialisms may be by type of study, such as:

Customer satisfaction.
Employee research.
Investor relations.
Social research.
Opinion polls.
Readership surveys.
Audience research.

Some agencies undertake only ad-hoc studies, whilst others carry out multi-client or syndicated studies, or publish research reports. The studies may be one-off or may be continuous (in order to track trends). There are also specialist agencies that undertake retail audits or omnibus studies.

Research agencies may be local, national or international in their range of operations. The size of the agency, in terms of number of employees or resources at their disposal, will affect the scale of the projects they are able to undertake.

The level of service offered by the research agency may range from "full service" (meaning they offer all stages of a research project), to those offering specialist services, such as fieldwork only (offering only the interviewing stage), "field and tab" (offering the interviews plus data analysis), or just data processing. These are described more fully below:

- **Full-service agencies** will be able to provide professional staff to design your project (i.e. to decide what needs doing), but will also be able to provide professional staff to collect, analyse and evaluate the data.

- **Consultants** offer a range of services, but most of them are qualitative specialists. Some offer both qualitative and quantitative research and will subcontract out those elements of the work they are unable to do themselves (such as quantitative interviewing or large-scale data analysis).

- **Fieldwork and tabulation** agencies deal with data collection and data analysis. They may have a team of face-to-face interviewers and/or a telephone interviewing centre. "Fieldwork" basically means the interviewing process, and "tabulation" means producing tables (computer print-outs) of the data generated by the survey.

- **Data preparation and analysis** agencies do not do fieldwork but undertake various types of computer analysis.

The Market Research Society offers a Research Buyers Guide (www.rbg.org.uk) to help companies' find practitioners who comply with their Code of Conduct. They categorise their members into five areas:

- Full-service agencies.

- Freelance consultants.

- Fieldwork and tabulation services.

- Data preparation and analysis.

- Group discussion and viewing facilities.

Activity 5.2

Just as an example, think of a specific type of survey you or your organisation might commission. Draw up a specification of the characteristics you would look for in an agency. For this activity you should think about the purpose and type of data you want to gather. The selection of a research agency is discussed in more detail in the next Session.

The marketing research process

Marketing research is carried out both continuously and on an ad-hoc basis, and underpins the marketing plans of any organisation. For example, a full marketing audit includes an analysis of the external environment on a continuous basis, as well as ad-hoc updates of customers' changing needs.

Marketing research undertaken on an ad-hoc basis is usually carried out to support specific marketing activities, such as the launch of a new product or entry into a new market.

The marketing research process is clear and is structured as follows:

1. Define the research problem

Initial exploratory research helps define the problem and can help in forming hypotheses. This stage can also help assess whether expensive research is justified.

2. **Set the objectives for the research**

    A clear objective will focus the direction of the research, and will help those responsible to ensure the results are valid and reliable.

3. **Construct the research proposal**

    This is particularly important if the research is to be carried out by an external agency, but also serves a purpose when for instance an individual in the marketing department carries out research on someone else's behalf. It ensures that there is full agreement on how the research will progress and what the likely costs are.

4. **Specify data collection methodology**

    What technique or combination of techniques will be used to collect the data?

5. **Select the sample**

    This important stage is discussed in more detail in Session 13. It is extremely rare that marketers can afford to research the whole of the relevant population, so accurate sampling is incredibly important and can make the difference between the success or failure of the research.

6. **Undertake some preliminary desk research**

7. **Define the questions to be asked**

    Design the questionnaire and pilot it to identify any weaknesses.

8. **Collect the data**

    The action stage of the process.

9. **Analyse and interpret the findings of the research**

10. **Present the results**

    Once sense has been made of the data collected, it then needs to be presented in a suitable format for the users of the research. This is often a formal report and a presentation with question and answer session.

As with any process, setting clear objectives at the beginning of the plan will help to ensure that it succeeds.

Activity 5.3

List the stages of the marketing research process. Make brief notes explaining what each stage of the process involves. This activity will assist you in answering the third Case Study question.

Case Study

(This Case Study is also used in Sessions 6 and 12.)

Cromwell's Breads Ltd.

Background

Mike Cromwell is the Marketing Manager of Cromwell's Breads Ltd., a medium sized regional bakery in Shropshire that was established in 1938 by Mike's grandfather, Tom. The company bakes and sells a number of well-known brands of bread under licensing arrangements, as well as its own label products. For the last 30 years, since Tom retired, the firm has been run by Sam Cromwell, Mike's father. It sells to retail shops, restaurants and institutions (schools, hospitals etc.).

Mike has been involved in the bread business all his life. As a boy he cleaned up at the bakery, and then later worked as a van driver/salesman during college holidays. After gaining his qualification in marketing, Mike began to work full-time for the company. After a couple of years in the office, his father appointed him Retail Sales Manager in charge of 24 drivers/salesmen. A year later he was put in charge of retail and commercial accounts and took the title Marketing Manager.

The problem

About three years ago Cromwell's Breads introduced a speciality line called Cromwell's Health Bread. Speciality bread is made from special or mixed grain flour and is heavier than regular bread. Not only have speciality breads been a rapidly growing segment of the bread market, they are also higher gross margin products. Industry trade publications identified the speciality bread consumer as coming from upper-income households and more highly educated than the typical bread consumer.

Mike knew that Cromwell's speciality breads were high quality and that they should be selling well, however the sales figures indicated otherwise. Cromwell's

Health Line seemed to be rapidly losing market share to the national brands, whilst it was clear that the major supermarket chains such as Sainsbury's and Tesco's were selling a lot of their own-label speciality breads. Cromwell's salespeople could offer no real insight into why their Health Line was doing so badly.

Mike decided to do something that he had never tried at Cromwell's Breads Ltd. before – marketing research. He knew he would have trouble selling the idea to his father, but he also knew that he needed more information. Taking out a pad of paper, Mike began making notes on what he would like to know about the position of Cromwell's Health Line. Except for his own sales records and reports in trade publications, he decided he knew very little.

He was unaware of the growth rate of the speciality bread market in his area. He had no idea who bought his bread or his competitors, or how much consumers bought and how often. He didn't know who in the household asked for speciality bread or selected the brand. Another point that troubled him was not knowing the relative awareness of Cromwell's Health and its image among consumers. Finally, he hadn't been on a delivery route for some time and he thought he should get a better idea of retailers' attitudes towards Cromwell's Health Line.

Source: this Case is fictitious and has been written for educational purposes only.

Questions

1. Advise Mike of the different types of market research practitioners that could help him.

2. Make a recommendation as to the factors he should consider when selecting the most suitable type of agency.

3. Explain to Mike the various stages in the marketing research process, ensuring that he understands the importance of each stage.

SUMMARY OF KEY POINTS

In this Session we have introduced the industry and process of marketing research and covered the following key points:

- The market research industry is made up of full-service agencies, specialist service agencies, field agencies, data analysis services and independent consultants.

- The industry is self-regulated by professional bodies such as the Market Research Society.

- The stages of the research process are:

  - Define the research problem.

  - Set the objectives for the research.

  - Construct the research proposal.

  - Specify the data collection methodology.

  - Select the sample.

  - Collect and analyse data.

  - Present the results.

Improving and developing own learning

The following projects are designed to help you develop your knowledge and skills further, by carrying out some research yourself. Feedback is not provided for this type of learning because there are no "answers" to be found, but you may wish to discuss your findings with colleagues and fellow students.

Project A

Visit the following web sites and identify the key issues they include in their Codes of Practice.

www.mrs.org.uk

www.esomar.org

Project B

Visit the following web sites and identify the types of research offered by these full-service agencies.

www.bmrb.co.uk

www.nopworld.com

Project C

Talk to your colleagues in the Marketing Department and identify:

- What information is sourced internally.
- What information is sourced via market research specialists.

Feedback to activities

Activity 5.1

There are 34 companies claiming to offer a general national omnibus, 21 that offer an omnibus in Financial Services.

The Code of Conduct guidelines of the Market Research Society covers such issues as privacy, data protection and human rights. The guidelines are regularly updated.

Activity 5.2

You answer will be related to the survey you chose. For an IT company carrying out an international survey your criteria may be similar to the following:

'We need a research company that can undertake fieldwork in five main countries in Europe (UK, France, Germany, Italy and the Netherlands). We want both telephone and personal interviews to be carried out in the native language. The completed interviews need to be submitted in English. We need 50 interviews per country but we have a tight (four week) deadline. We need an agency that can undertake the above and has experience in working in the IT industry. Ideally we would like to have some contact names to take up references. We want a shortlist of four companies that meet the above criteria.'

Activity 5.3

You should have explained each stage using brief notes.

The stages are as follows:

Define the research problem.

Set the objectives for the research.

Construct the research proposal.

Specify data collection methodology.

Select the sample.

Design and pilot the questionnaire.

Collect the data.

Analyse the findings.

Write the report.

Present the results.

Session 6

Selecting and briefing marketing research suppliers

Introduction

This Session is the first to look at the practical issues of marketing research, starting with the criteria for selecting an appropriate agency. It goes on to consider how information for specific decisions might be identified, and then looks at how an effective research brief can be produced.

LEARNING OUTCOMES

At the end of this Session you will be able to:

- Describe the procedures for selecting a marketing research supplier.

- Identify information requirements to support a specific business decision in an organisation.

- Develop a research brief to meet the specific requirements of a marketing decision.

Commissioning research

In the last Session we looked at the various types of agency and marketing research practitioner that might be used by an organisation. Once this part of the selection process has been made, then other factors can influence which of the competing firms is selected to carry out the research.

An internal brief for marketing research will help the commissioners (that is the organisation) to gain clarity about the problem they are trying to solve and the objectives of their research. Without this specification the goal posts are likely to keep changing, giving rise to unrealistic expectations from both the company and the research agency performing the project.

Research agencies will often be sent an outline specification in advance of the first meeting, so that the agency selection process can begin with detailed pitches about their credentials and chosen methodologies for the project. Once the agencies have been chosen a fuller briefing and refining of the specification and objectives can then take place.

When you have reached this stage you will be able to prepare a draft research brief. This is the document that you will give to the research agencies and which will define the task for them. The more key information you can include in it, the more likely they are to give you a useful, constructive and appropriate response. The draft should therefore contain:

- A summary of the background to the research.

- An outline of the opportunities or problems that need to be explored and, in particular, details of what you want to do with the information once you get it.

- A description of the people whose views are of interest – the potential respondents.

- An outline of the questions that seem, at this early stage, to need answering.

- Suggestions on how the data might be collected.

- A description of what you are expecting to get. What are the "deliverables"? Advice only? Data? A full report?

- An indication of timing. When, being realistic, will the work be able to start, and when is the information needed by?

- An outline of any contractual requirements you would anticipate.

- A budget. How much money is likely to be available for the work?

- When do you need the agencies' proposals? (Remember to give them a reasonable amount of thinking and writing time.)

Don't forget to ask for an outline of the agency's (and its relevant staff's) experience.

Market research agencies may be chosen on the basis of a variety of criteria, such as:

- Experience with similar companies in the same sector.

- Track record with particular types of methodologies, for example telephone research.

- Capacity, resources and size of the agency, including national and international coverage.

- Credibility in the field, which helps to promote the validity of the research.

- Externality, which can enhance the objectivity of the research.

A meeting would be arranged with those marketing research agencies that demonstrate an ability to fulfil the initial brief. This would be an exploratory meeting so that the company can present its background and give an introduction to the problem to be solved. The agency would then question the company further about their needs before agreeing a time frame to produce a research proposal.

In response the marketing research agency would forward a proposal that outlines the following:

- The credentials of the agency.
- Their way of working.
- The objectives of the project.
- An outline of their process and methodologies.
- A timetable and milestones.
- The budget.

One of the main concerns of any organisation is the rapport between the agency staff and the marketing team. PR companies used to be notorious for presenting senior account staff at the briefing stage only to replace them, once the contract had been won, with junior members who had no relationship with the client company. It is important at these early stages to form a relationship with an ongoing contact who will manage the project.

The project will be monitored and evaluated not only on the outcome of the findings, but also on the performance of the agency. There need to be performance objectives (including timetabling and budgeting) to assess the performance of the agency. Milestones, set at discreet intervals, can help with the monitoring of the project. For example, it may be that in phase one of a project a database of individuals from organisations needs to be created so that a questionnaire can then be sent by post; without this stage of the process being completed successfully the whole project will stall. The use of project management software such as Microsoft Project can help to keep everyone informed of the agreed timescales.

Activity 6.1

Taking a problem in your work place that needs to be solved through the collection of information, list the key information requirements and identify

---

> possible sources for secondary research (sources of information are discussed in more detail in Session 9).

Information to support business decisions

Organisations make decisions on a daily basis, which may well have commercial, ethical and socio-cultural implications. An organisation might decide to introduce a new product into its portfolio despite having little or no previous experience on which to base their decision on, as was the case with the Sony Walkman.

When Sony took the decision to produce a new "object" that would play music, without the facility to record, and which used headphones so that the experience was entirely personal, could they have known how successful the product would become? Would retailers immediately know its value and sing its praises? Could Sony have known that this product would be a trendsetter and its uses would become a way of life for young and old alike?

What kind of information would Sony have needed to collect to support their decision to produce the Walkman?

Sony's information needs would have been:

- Profile of the likely purchaser, including age, income group and occupation.

- Existing distribution network and its ability to meet demand led by marketing campaign.

- Media opportunities related to target audience habits.

- Possible uses for the Sony Walkman, for example when might the product be used e.g. travelling, walking, running, in the gym, etc.

- Price comparisons with competing products, such as Hi-Fis, portable radios etc.

These information needs would have helped Sony build up a picture of the marketing mix they would need, allowing them to evaluate the investment needed to fulfil the project. However, it's not just production and marketing costs that need to be considered, so an internal audit would also need to take place, looking at the:

- Financial implications for investment and working capital.

- Staffing costs in all relevant departments.

- Marketing budget for launch, distribution incentives and ongoing advertising.

- Internal training and briefings to introduce the product internally.

- Production and material costs.

- Logistics and servicing implications and resources.

- Internal organisational structure and culture.

- Capital costs, including manufacturing plant and equipment.

When an organisation takes the decision to produce a new product it has far-reaching implications, and there is always some risk attached. Putting together a business case can be a costly investment, and sometimes the product never makes it to production. However, it is better to have the information before you to make that decision, rather than blindly carrying on and hoping it will be a success.

Activity 6.2

Consider a recent decision made by your organisation, or one that is about to be made. List the implications both internally and externally of insufficient research into stakeholder needs. How could this situation be improved by researching people's needs?

The research brief

The research brief needs to outline the background to the enquiry and the basic needs of the research project, complete with clear objectives against which the project will be measured.

The brief acts as a plan of action for both the commissioning organisation and the agency. Possible contents include:

- Frame the research problem.

- Formulate the key objectives.

- Determine supporting knowledge.

- Develop specific questions or queries.

- Select a methodology.

- Set the boundaries for enquiry.

- Describe the data collection process.
- State the required outcomes.
- Budget and timetable.
- Ethical considerations.

Framing the research problem means identifying the areas of enquiry that require further systematic investigation. What do you need to know? How will the information be used once the project is complete? These questions are important in guiding the width and breadth of the enquiry.

Formulating the key objectives provides a framework of enquiry that guides the outcomes of the project, making evaluation easier.

Determining supporting knowledge. This element of the process requires a critical review of any existing studies that concern the area of enquiry. This will help the researcher frame the area of new enquiry needed, and help them build up knowledge of the topic area. The findings will also help support the interpretation of the results.

Developing specific questions or queries helps to set the direction of the study, so that the target audience can be identified and different methodologies examined.

Selecting a methodology is the most fundamental aspect of the research process and defines the way in which the information will be collected. For example, will it be collected by face-to-face interviews or by a postal questionnaire?

Setting the boundaries for enquiry means that the length of the study and the sampling objectives are quantified, so that the project can meet the required business objectives within the specified time frame.

Describing the data collection process helps to identify possible milestones or any obstacles to success.

Stating the required outcomes helps everyone focus on what they are trying to achieve with the research and addresses how the findings might be presented. This might be in the form of a report, a presentation, or as database information.

Budget and timetable requirements need to be stated, as this information will affect the design of the project. For example, if a project has to be completed in three months, you would have to assess the likelihood of being able to access enough individuals for face-to-face interviews in time.

Ethical considerations need to be stated so that everyone contacted understands the scope and purpose of the study and can decide whether they wish to be involved or not.

Case Study

Cromwell's Breads Ltd.

Background

Mike Cromwell is the Marketing Manager of Cromwell's Breads Ltd., a medium sized regional bakery in Shropshire that was established in 1938 by Mike's grandfather, Tom. The company bakes and sells a number of well-known brands of bread under licensing arrangements, as well as its own label products. For the last 30 years, since Tom retired, the firm has been run by Sam Cromwell, Mike's father. It sells to retail shops, restaurants and institutions (schools, hospitals etc.).

Mike has been involved in the bread business all his life. As a boy he cleaned up at the bakery, and then later worked as a van driver/salesman during college holidays. After gaining his qualification in marketing, Mike began to work full-time for the company. After a couple of years in the office, his father appointed him Retail Sales Manager in charge of 24 drivers/salesmen. A year later he was put in charge of retail and commercial accounts and took the title Marketing Manager.

The problem

About three years ago Cromwell's Breads introduced a speciality line called Cromwell's Health Bread. Speciality bread is made from special or mixed grain flour and is heavier than regular bread. Not only have speciality breads been a rapidly growing segment of the bread market, they are also higher gross margin products. Industry trade publications identified the speciality bread consumer as coming from upper-income households and more highly educated than the typical bread consumer.

Mike knew that Cromwell's speciality breads were high quality and that they should be selling well, however the sales figures indicated otherwise. Cromwell's Health Line seemed to be rapidly losing market share to the national brands, whilst it was clear that the major supermarket chains such as Sainsbury's and Tesco's were selling a lot of their own-label speciality breads. Cromwell's salespeople could offer no real insight into why their Health Line was doing so badly.

Mike decided to do something that he had never tried at Cromwell's Breads Ltd. before – marketing research. He knew he would have trouble selling the idea to his father, but he also knew that he needed more information. Taking out a pad of paper, Mike began making notes on what he would like to know about the position of Cromwell's Health Line. Except for his own sales records and reports in trade publications, he decided he knew very little.

He was unaware of the growth rate of the speciality bread market in his area. He had no idea who bought his bread or his competitors, or how much consumers bought and how often. He didn't know who in the household asked for speciality bread or selected the brand. Another point that troubled him was not knowing the relative awareness of Cromwell's Health and its image among consumers. Finally, he hadn't been on a delivery route for some time and he thought he should get a better idea of retailers' attitudes towards Cromwell's Health Line.

Source: this Case Study is fictitious.

Questions

1. In the last Session you advised Mike on how he should decide on which **type** of marketing research practitioner to use. Now advise him on the other factors he will need to consider before selecting an agency.

2. Define the research problem that Cromwell's faces.

3. Write a research brief for Cromwell's current research needs.

SUMMARY OF KEY POINTS

In this Session we have examined the selection and briefing of marketing research suppliers and covered the following key points:

- External suppliers can be useful as they are usually more objective, have specialist skills and facilities, and often have more experience in the specific market/topic.

- Base research supplier selection on experience, technical expertise, resources, reputation, and communication and relationship skills.

- The research brief should include:

  - Framing the research problem.

  - Formulating the key objectives.

  - Determining supporting knowledge.

  - Developing specific questions or queries.

  - Selecting a methodology.

  - Setting the boundaries for enquiry.

  - Describing the data collection process.

  - Stating the required outcomes.

  - Budget and timetable.

  - Ethical considerations.

Improving and developing own learning

The following projects are designed to help you develop your knowledge and skills further, by carrying out some research yourself. Feedback is not provided for this type of learning because there are no "answers" to be found, but you may wish to discuss your findings with colleagues and fellow students.

Project A

Talk to colleagues in your Marketing Department about how decisions are made about who should carry out research. What factors influence whether or not research is undertaken, or whether it is done internally or externally?

Project B

Talk to colleagues in your Marketing Department and ask to see a research brief that has been used to commission research for a specific purpose. Make links to the sections suggested in the Session above. Could you improve the document?

Project C

Taking a research problem within your own organisation, write a research brief using the headings listed in this Session. Are there any additional information needs that prevent you from designing the brief? How would you overcome this problem?

Feedback to activities

Activity 6.1

If for example you wanted to conduct a study to evaluate the current attitudes to your products within your distributor network, you would need to first evaluate the distributors in terms of their volume of business to identify "groupings", such as geographical regions, length of business relationship etc.

Likely sources of secondary research include:

- Local or business libraries for reports, periodicals and articles.
- The Internet for company searches, annual reports and previous research materials.
- Archives for back copies of magazines, newspapers and reports.

Activity 6.2

Often internal decisions are made without considering other people's needs, both inside and outside the organisation. Building a map of likely needs can help to ensure commitment from all stakeholders. The map overleaf is an example of possible needs.

Stakeholder needs

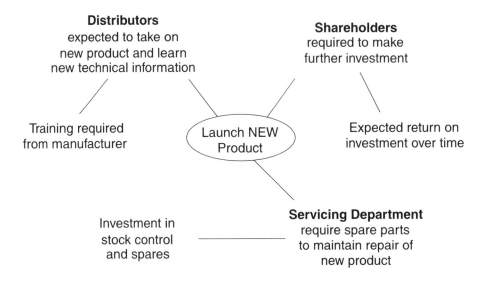

A lack of understanding of the needs of each stakeholder group will impact on their ability to carry out their work efficiently.

When decisions are made, the involvement of the right people is essential, so that:

- All the potential barriers to implementation are properly considered.

- Every departmental manager affected has the right information at the right time and can communicate this to their teams, enabling a common understanding.

- Everyone understands the importance of their contribution to the bigger picture.

- Everyone can plan effectively, knowing the impact the decision will have on their current and future priorities.

You may have identified other issues or specific issues relating to the decision you selected.

Session 7

Market research proposals

Introduction

This Session builds on the last, in that it considers the research proposal and how it is prepared to meet a given brief. It also considers the essential areas of ethical and legislative issues that impact on the research process.

LEARNING OUTCOMES

At the end of this Session you will be able to:

- Develop a research proposal to fulfil a given research brief.

- Explain the ethical and social responsibilities inherent in the market research task.

- Describe the key legislation that impacts on the marketing research process.

The research proposal

The research proposal defines what the research agency promises to do for the client, the timescale and the budget. It is said to be the most important element of the marketing research process. The proposal should take the form of a report in writing, outlining the research process and the expected outcomes, as per the brief.

The proposal is likely to include the following:

1. Background of the customer organisation, showing an understanding of the context and the problem.

2. Objectives for the project and the expected outcomes.

3. Methodology and the process of research.

4. Timetable, with milestones so that the project can be monitored and managed successfully.

5. Budget and terms and conditions.

Three or four agencies are normally asked to make a proposal. Proposal writing is a time-consuming and therefore costly exercise, so it is unfair to ask firms to do this work if they have less than about a one in four chance of getting the job. Besides, proposal costs have to be recouped within the agencies' income, so excessive requests for proposals will eventually increase the overall cost of research.

When selecting an agency, clients should look out for the following points:

a. If the proposal is vague, be aware that the outcomes may also be unclear. Proposals should state clearly who is responsible for the project, what will be done by when, and how the results will be presented.

b. Research jargon can confuse, and it is the role of the agency to make the proposal understandable for the client.

c. Anything not stated will not be provided, so check assumptions.

A proposal might look like this:

Proposal for the analysis of likely sales of sunglasses in Europe

Background

The clients' laboratory has developed a new design of flexible frames for their range of sunglasses, which means that the product is more durable and the design more comfortable for the wearer.

The company already distributes a range of sunglasses through opticians in Europe and would now like to branch out into the fashion sunglasses market.

Objectives

To forecast the demand for the new flexi-frame product in 10 European countries.

To identify a new distribution network in the retail fashion market.

To map the structure of the market for retail sunglasses.

To forecast sales of the new flexi range for the next 3 years.

Methodology

1. Desk research will establish what statistics and information is available for market size in European countries, including import and export data, purchasing patterns for sunglasses, channels of distribution, competitive data, and other information related to the objectives.

2. Field research will include visits to retailers in the UK, Germany, France and Spain to establish prices at the point of sale of the most fashionable brands identified in the competitor research.

3. Field research with six retail chain buyers in the UK, Germany, France and Spain, to identify mark-ups, suppliers, negotiation process, etc.

4. Consumer research will be carried out with a random sample of 20 individuals in each country to identify buying criteria, habits and attitudes.

Timetable

Phase 1:   Desk research (November to December).
Phase 2:   Field research in European countries (January to February).
Phase 3:   Focus groups in European countries (March).
Phase 4:   Report writing and presentation of results (April).

Milestone

The product must be in a suitable state to demonstrate at the focus group meetings – this is a resource requirement that is required at a key time in the timetable.

Budget

The question of cost is not covered in detail in this brief introduction because there are so many variables involved. For example:

- How many questions need answering?

- How difficult will it be to contact the respondents?

- How many interviews will be required?

- How complex is the analysis?

- Is a presentation of the data required?

All of these variables will affect the eventual cost of the research project.

(The budget should give a detailed breakdown of all costs and expenses.)

Activity 7.1

Prepare a presentation for your Manager explaining the process of commissioning an agency to undertake a research project, and how you will decide which agency is awarded the contract. You might want to look back at your answer to Activity 5.2 in Session 5.

Legal and ethical issues

Is it legal and is it ethical?

Market research is a process for obtaining information to improve decision making and for analysing customer needs and wants. Intrusions on privacy are a major concern, and both the way in which questions are asked and the type of information sought are sensitive areas for the researcher.

No information that might identify the informants should be revealed to the company commissioning the research and under no circumstances should names and addresses be combined with survey results.

Also, results should never be biased towards an expected outcome. This can happen when the researcher uses leading questions or when samples are chosen from a group that is most likely to agree or disagree with certain questions.

Questionable practices used to elicit information about the competition through devious means, such as hidden cameras or using student projects to obtain information, also raise ethical questions.

Selling and marketing under the guise of research is covered by strict guidelines. Visit www.esomar.org for more information on this.

Activity 7.2

Describe six ways in which competitor information can be sought without resorting to unethical tactics.

Codes of conduct

Research depends on the co-operation of the public. The industry, both clients and agencies, relies on people giving up their time to be interviewed and thus providing information about what they do and what they would like. Not surprisingly, there are rules about what the research industry can, and cannot, do in collecting this sort of data.

There is legislation that sets some limits, and the Market Research Society (MRS), like all professional bodies, has a **Code of Conduct** for its members. At this stage all you really need to know is that the foundation stone of these rules is that nobody who provides information should be misled about what they are involved in. So, to give one example of the rules, if a confidential survey research project is carried out, there must not be any follow-up sales calls to those who have been interviewed – it is research only.

The onus is on the research agency to ensure that nothing is done which conflicts with the MRS Code of Conduct. The full Code is included on the Research Buyers Guide (RBG) CD-ROM (see Codes of Conduct) and also on the MRS web site (www.mrs.org.uk).

ESOMAR also encourages research agencies to adopt codes of practice to prevent companies using research to sell and market products. The increased visibility of the contribution of research to business decisions underlines the need for self-regulation and quality standards. Although the industry remains largely self-regulated, in some countries legislation has been adopted to provide additional protection to the privacy of members of the public, such as the Data Protection Act (1998) in the UK.

Members of CASRO (Council of American Survey Research Organisations), and the MRA (Marketing Research Association) have undertaken to abide by the ICC/ESOMAR International Code of Marketing and Social Research Practice that is applied by 100 associations worldwide.

This Code takes into account privacy regulations and sets out the core principles governing researchers' relations with respondents, with clients, and with other researchers. Key principles are that respondents co-operation is always voluntary, that their confidentiality should be maintained, and that marketing research activities must be clearly differentiated from direct marketing activities.

The following **Rights of Respondents** has been copied from the ESOMAR web site (www.esomar.org), under the Rules section of the ICC/ESOMAR International Code of Marketing and Social Research Practice Guidelines.

1. Respondents' co-operation in a marketing research project is entirely voluntary at all stages. They must not be misled when being asked for their co-operation.

2. Respondents' anonymity must be strictly preserved. If the Respondent on request from the Researcher has given permission for data to be passed on in a form which allows that Respondent to be personally identified:

    a. the Respondent must first have been told to whom the information would be supplied and the purposes for which it will be used, and also

    b. the Researcher must ensure that the information will not be used for any non-research purpose and that the recipient of the information has agreed to conform to the requirements of this Code.

3. The Researcher must take all reasonable precautions to ensure that Respondents are in no way directly harmed or adversely affected as a result of their participation in a marketing research project.

4. The Researcher must take special care when interviewing children and young people. The informed consent of the parent or responsible adult must first be obtained for interviews with children.

5. Respondents must be told (normally at the beginning of the interview) if observation techniques or recording equipment are being used, except where these are used in a public place. If a Respondent so wishes, the record or relevant section of it must be destroyed or deleted. Respondents' anonymity must not be infringed by the use of such methods.

6. Respondents must be enabled to check without difficulty the identity and bona fides of the Researcher.

Case Study

Belts and Braces

Research brief

Background

Belts and Braces have been making belts for the clothing industry in the UK since 1950. They are based in the East Midlands, and started off with many clients who are major UK retailers. However, recently the management have realised that they are increasingly reliant on a few major key accounts. While this does not pose an immediate threat to the company, there is a need to diversify risk through expansion of the client portfolio and to grow the business into new segments and geographic markets. With this in mind, the company would like to investigate the UK market for retail belts (as opposed to Original Equipment Manufacturers, OEMs).

Objectives

The UK retail belts market is a complex one, with both domestic and foreign products playing an important role. Given this fact, it is vitally important that Belts and Braces have a thorough understanding of the shape and dynamics of the market, so that they are able to develop an appropriate marketing strategy to both enter and develop the market. The primary objective of this research is to analyse the structure of the UK retail belt market in terms of the size of the market, the predominant market segments and their consumer profiles, the major competitors in each (and their relative strengths and weaknesses), the primary channels of distribution, the pricing structures and promotional techniques.

The secondary objective of the research is to canvas the opinion of consumers in the major segments as to their preferences when buying belts in terms of price, quality, type of retail outlet, styling, sizes, colours and utility. This will give Belts and Braces a better understanding of the purchasing criteria that motivates the individual, and this information can then be used to inform marketing strategy decisions.

Information requirements

Based on the above objectives, the information requirements for this study are as follows:

1. The size, structure and dynamics of the UK market for retail belts.

2. A comprehensive list of competitors in each segment of the retail belt market, with analysis of strengths and weaknesses (of the companies and their products).

3. A comprehensive analysis of the major channels of distribution (retail), which would be appropriate for Belts and Braces products.

4. A study of the consumer profiles of customers in each of the major market segments.

5. A study of 20 consumers' purchasing criteria in each of the major segments.

Structure

The research is to fall into two phases. The first phase should comprise of the "macro" market research elements (up to and including point 4 in the above information requirements). At that point in the research there will be a review period during which Belts and Braces should decide on which market segments it wishes to develop further. Once those segments have been chosen, phase 2 of the research can begin.

Timescale

The timescale for the research is three months.

Contact

For further information on this research brief please contact Eddie Birch at Belts and Braces.

Source: this Case is fictitious and has been written for educational purposes only.

Questions

1. Identify any further questions you would want to ask the company before preparing the proposal.

2. Prepare a proposal in response to the brief from Belts and Braces.

SUMMARY OF KEY POINTS

In this Session we have introduced marketing research proposals and covered the following key points:

- The research proposal is said to be the most important of the whole research project.

- The proposal is based on the brief given and provides a template and contract for the project.

- The proposal should contain:

  - Background.

  - Objectives.

  - Methodology.

  - Timescales.

  - Budget.

- The research industry depends on goodwill, trust, professionalism and confidentiality.

- It is governed by the data protection legislation of the country in which companies operate, but is primarily a self-regulated industry.

Improving and developing own learning

The following projects are designed to help you develop your knowledge and skills further, by carrying out some research yourself. Feedback is not provided for this type of learning because there are no "answers" to be found, but you may wish to discuss your findings with colleagues and fellow students.

Project A

Talk to colleagues in your Marketing Department and ask to see some research briefs that have been prepared, together with the proposals that resulted from them. See if you can identify which one was selected as the winning proposal. Were you correct? What made it stand out? If you did not correctly identify the winning proposal, talk to your colleagues about what other factors affected the decision.

Project B

If possible, arrange to sit in on a presentation to your organisation of a proposal by a research agency. What does the presentation add to the written proposal?

Project C

Talk to people within your organisation who prepare project proposals. Discuss why it is useful to work within a Code of Conduct. If you have not prepared a proposal yourself, work shadow a colleague who is currently preparing one.

Feedback to activities

Activity 7.1

Market research agencies may be chosen on the basis of a variety of criteria, such as:

- Which company seems to have understood what you need?

- Which company has perhaps added to your thinking by coming up with ideas of their own?

- Does the proposed research design seem to match your expectations and, if not, are convincing alternatives presented and explained?

- Does the company have relevant experience, either in terms of methodology and/or the subject of your project?

- Assuming that they have understood your needs, do they seem to be offering value for money?

- Which company's work "feels right"? From your contacts with the agency and from the documents it has produced for you, do you think you trust the organisation and can work with its' staff?

- Has the agency a track record with particular types of methodologies, for example telephone research?

- How well resourced is the agency? Does it have national and international coverage?

- What profile does the agency have with the media? Using a company like Mori will help to promote the validity of the research.

Activity 7.2

Your answer should have included six of the sources listed below.

Competitor information can be obtained ethically from:

- Internet searches.

- Promotional materials.

- Annual reports.

- Trade journals.

- National and regional newspapers.

- Sales force feedback.

- Trade directories.

- Company brochures.

- Industry directories.

- Stockbroker reports.

- Trade shows.

- Financial/credit rating services.

- Market reports.

Session 8

Secondary data

Introduction

This Session examines secondary data (also known as desk research) in detail. It looks at its uses, its benefits and its limitations.

LEARNING OUTCOMES

At the end of this Session you will be able to:

- Explain the uses of secondary data.
- Explain the benefits of secondary data.
- Explain the limitations of secondary data.

Secondary research

Secondary research, which is also referred to as desk research, involves the investigation of data that already exists. It may take the form of internal records, or might be reports that have been collated for another purpose.

Once the analyst has been tasked with a specific project, as much information is gathered in the first two or three weeks so that a proposal can be made to solve the problem. The information gained at this stage can also help with the development of questionnaires for primary research.

Desk research involves searching statistics, books, trade journals, the Internet and other reports for information on the selected market. Examples of places to look include:

- Libraries.
- Trade Associations.
- Exhibitions.
- Government departments.
- Banks.
- Stockbrokers.

- Competitors.
- Internet.

Examples of materials to search include:

- Trade journals.
- Trade directories.
- Market reports.
- Catalogues.
- Statistics.
- Technical reports.
- Lists.
- News articles.
- Financial reports.

A list of key words and phrases can be developed which may help the analyst search libraries, CD-ROMs and Internet sources for information pertinent to the project.

Why conduct desk research?

There are many reasons for gathering information that already exists. It enables a researcher to:

- Understand the product and the environment before beginning the research.
- Undertake a much more useful briefing meeting.
- Use the most appropriate definitions and terminology when researching the market.
- Select a suitable sample.
- Design a much better questionnaire.
- Be more successful in setting up interviews.
- Keep conversation flowing in telephone interviews.
- Include relevant material in a report.
- Communicate confidently the presentation of findings.

Consider the use you make of existing information. You are probably already aware of the main limitation of using existing material, which is that the information may not be in a suitable format for your requirements. Also it may be incomplete, because the original purpose was significantly different to the one driving your research.

Activity 8.1

Carry out a piece of secondary research by making a comparison of two major sports web sites. Your objective is to check the information provided to key audiences (such as coaches and individuals).

Benefits of secondary research

Secondary research is usually undertaken before any primary research, as it is much cheaper, and is often less time consuming, particularly with so much information now available on the Internet.

Exploratory research often takes place during the specification process, widening the knowledge base so that any gaps in information often present themselves. These gaps can then be filled by primary research.

Activity 8.2

Put together a short presentation to the marketing team explaining why secondary research might be undertaken before primary research.

Limitations of secondary research

Consideration needs to be given to how applicable the data is. Marketers need to remember that secondary data has not been gathered for the specific purpose they are now considering, so therefore there are limitations to its use. It may for instance be old and outdated. Research is used to predict the future, but markets can change very quickly, so marketing decision making must rely on the most recent statistics and information. Also, the information may only be available in a different format than the one required. In addition to all of these, comparability can be a difficult issue if the purpose of your research is significantly different to that of the original survey you are using.

Depending on the research objective, there may be no secondary data available. For example, when considering entry into a new international market, there is likely to be information available on the economic situation of the country, but investigating prospective customers' attitudes towards your products and services is likely to require primary research.

A final factor for consideration is the accuracy of the available data. Researchers need to assess the credibility of the source of the data, when it was gathered, and for what purpose. The method of collection and the sample size is also relevant.

In summary, marketers need to carefully evaluate any secondary data before using it. Main considerations include:

- Check the source. Might bias be an issue?
- Why was it collected?
- How was it collected?
- When was it collected? How old is the data?
- Be wary of just one "expert" view. Compare relevant information from different sources.
- Is the data comparable with your needs?

Here are some guidelines on using secondary information:

- Identify the key information required.
- Allow enough time to collect the information you need.
- Consider the budget. Even seemingly "free" resources incur cost, whether manpower or photocopying.
- Think laterally. A number of search terms may be needed to locate the relevant information.
- Attribute sources to gain credibility.
- Does it seem right? What is your gut feel? Just because it has been published somewhere else does not necessarily mean that it is correct.
- Keep a working file of useful information.

Activity 8.3

Prepare three slides explaining the main limitations of secondary data and how each might be overcome.

Case Study

Glass blocks

Joe Denver works as a Research Executive for a full-service agency in London, UK. He was recently asked to investigate the market for glass blocks (large, heavy-duty and decorative blocks for use in the building industry) in the UK. He specifically wanted information about the market size, trends, the main suppliers, types of product available (together with pricing information if available), and examples of how the product is used and who the main users might be.

His finished report impressed his Manager, who has asked him to use it to demonstrate the usefulness of secondary data at the Induction Training for new staff next week.

Unfortunately, Joe cannot now access the report, and does not want to let his Manager know that he has lost his copy. He has found the following notes about where information can be obtained and in what format.

Locations

British Library.
National Statistics Office.
Internet.
Building Centre.

Publications

Barbour Index Directory.
Exhibition Bulletin.
BRAD.
Willings Press Guide.
Directory of Associations.
Directory of Special Libraries and Information Centres.
Building Trade Directory.
Findex (directory of market studies).

Organisations

Architects Association.
Royal Institute of British Architects.
Stockbrokers.
Banks.

Information needed

Names of companies specifying the product.
Import and export data.
Recent and relevant exhibitions and trade shows.
Financial information about the five key players in the market.
Recent projects involving the product.
Technical data.
Market studies.
Price information.
Industry trends.
Economic data.

Source: this Case is fictitious and has been written for educational purposes only.

Questions

Use the notes above to identify the reason that Joe used:

1.   Each location.

2.   Each publication.

3.   Each organisation.

Explain what part of his information needs each might be used to satisfy.

SUMMARY OF KEY POINTS

In this Session we have introduced secondary data and covered the following key points:

■ Secondary data is information that has been previously gathered for some purpose other than the current project.

■ It helps to clarify the information requirements, enables more insightful interpretation of primary data, provides comparative data, and provides information that cannot be obtained through primary research.

- Secondary data is faster and less expensive to collect than primary data – the Internet has made this much more so.
- Sources of secondary data include:
  - Sales figures.
  - Operational data.
  - Customer satisfaction results.
  - Advertising spend.
  - Evaluations of previous campaigns.
  - Customer complaints records.
  - Research reports from previous studies.
  - Internet.
  - Directories.
  - Published reports.
  - News sources.
- Its limitations include availability, applicability, accuracy and comparability.
- Its use should be evaluated before starting research.

Improving and developing own learning

The following projects are designed to help you develop your knowledge and skills further, by carrying out some research yourself. Feedback is not provided for this type of learning because there are no "answers" to be found, but you may wish to discuss your findings with colleagues and fellow students.

Project A

Talk to colleagues in your Marketing Department about the sources of secondary data they use on a regular basis. Can you add to their list of useful sources?

Project B

Search the Internet for information about your three main competitors. How much information can you find about their products, their prices, their promotional activity, their channels to market and their plans for the future?

Project C

Make a library or Internet search to find market reports that are relevant to your organisation (Mintel, Keynote etc.). When were these reports prepared?

Feedback to activities

Activity 8.1

You may have chosen one or two of the following sports. Examples of comparison of six major sports web sites.

	Coaches	Individuals	Headings	Any stand out
Swimming	Good.	Very good, comprehensive information.	Some could be clearer.	Nothing particularly.
Rounders	Easy to find, with wealth of information.	Easy, comprehensive.	Good headings.	Nothing exciting.
Gymnastics	Easy to find – few links.	Not easy to find information about clubs for individuals.	Poor.	Quite a simple site.
Hockey	Very good, online help.	Not good.	Vague.	Good, eye-catching, e.g. Commonwealth Games link.
Tennis	Very comprehensive.	Players Zone – long list of titles. FAQs particularly good.	Very clear, a good site.	Links for shirts etc.
Netball	Best information, gave details of different courses.	List of telephone numbers to contact.	Good – but information hopelessly outdated.	Nothing.

	Overall impression	Membership information	Schools	Clubs
Swimming	Classy colours, but dull. Good, up-to-date news.	No, page not available and not obvious.	Not easy.	Very easy and comprehensive.
Rounders	Light and airy. No news. Very technical site.	Very easy to find on home page. Has all benefits clearly stated in list.	Can click straight into form to print off.	Not immediately obvious.
Gymnastics	Plain, but good animation. Up-to-date news available.	Easy to find, comprehensive.	No obvious schools membership, only pre-school.	No obvious clubs information.
Hockey	Clear, clean site. Plain.	Not at all obvious. Search produced nothing.	Not at all obvious.	Easy to find clubs in any area.
Tennis	Good home page. Very up-to-date news, but no link back to home page.	Easy to find, comprehensive. Can download application form.	Schools Zone – easy and comprehensive, can download application form.	Club Zone – but not easy to find details of membership.
Netball	Classy looking site, pleasing on the eye.	Not at all obvious where to go from home page.	Couldn't find.	No information, just a list of contacts to telephone.

	Swimming	Tennis	Hockey	Rounders	Gymnastics	Netball
Awards information	✓	✓	✗	✓	✓	✓
Technical guide	✓	✓	✗	✓	✗	✗
A Level/GCSE info/ Nat Curriculum	✓	✗	✗	✗	✗	✗
Sport rules	✓	✓	✗	✓	✗	✗
Coaching information	✓	✓	✓	✓	✓	✓
Funding help	✓	✓	✗	✗	✗	✓
Umpiring	✓	✓	✓	✓	✓	✓
News	✓	✓	✓	✓	✓ ★	✓
Clubs	✓	✓	✓	✗	✓	✓
Clubs newsletter	✓	✗	✗	✗	✗	✗
Web site guidelines	✓	✓	✗	✗	✗	✗
Insurance	✓	✗	✗	✗	✓	✗
Legal	✓	✗	✗	✗	✗	✗
Business plan	✓	✓	✗	✗	✗	✗
Annual report	✓	✓	✗	✗	✗	✗
Job vacancies	✓	✓	✗	✗	✗	✓

	Swimming	Tennis	Hockey	Rounders	Gymnastics	Netball
Site search	✓	✗	✗	✗	✗	✗
FAQs	✗	✓	✗	✗	✗	✓
Events guide	✓	✓	✓	✓	✓	✓
Links to other sites	✓	✓	✓	✗	✓	✓
Online shop	✗	✓	✗	✗	✓	✗
Chat zone	✗	✗	✓	✗	✗	✗

★ There, but hopelessly out of date.

Activity 8.2

> ### Secondary research
>
> - Also known as desk research.
> - Usually carried out before primary research.
> - Obtained from information sources that already exist.
> - It is therefore cheaper than primary research.
> - It is also quicker and easier to collect.

> ### Secondary research
>
> - Can be used to clarify information requirements.
> - Enables a more insightful interpretation of primary data.
> - Provides comparative data.
> - Provides information that cannot be obtained through primary research.

Activity 8.3

**Limitations of secondary research:
applicability**

- Is secondary data available?

- Is it available in the same format as we need?

- Is the information up to date?

**Limitations of secondary research:
accuracy**

- What credibility has the organisation undertaking the work?

- How reliable is the data?

- Was the method used suitable?

- Was the sample size suitable?

**Limitations of secondary research:
comparability**

- Why was it collected?

- How often are studies undertaken?

- What were the units of measurement?

- What were the situation and circumstances?

Session 9

Using primary and secondary data

Introduction

This Session looks at sources of primary data, and then how both primary and secondary data might be used in action.

LEARNING OUTCOMES

At the end of this Session you will be able to:

- Recognise the key sources of primary data.

- Give examples of primary data in action.

- Give examples of secondary data in action.

Primary research

Primary data is collected first-hand, specifically to meet the objectives of a research brief. This is in contrast to data gathered as a result of secondary research, which may answer some parts of the brief but was originally collected for another purpose.

Primary research, also known as field research, can be conducted in a number of ways. The three main methods are face to face, telephone and self-complete. Face-to-face interviews are also known as personal interviews if they are conducted one-to-one, or where a group of participants is involved they may be referred to as focus groups or workshops.

Information sourced through either secondary or primary techniques is either qualitative or quantitative. These terms are defined as follows:

Qualitative information

This is information that cannot be measured or expressed in numeric terms. It is useful to the marketer as it often explores people's feelings and opinions.

Quantitative information

In contrast, this is information that can be measured and expressed in numeric terms. For example, the percentage market share held, the number of customers buying our product in a certain month, or the number of sales calls made in a week.

Primary research techniques

Self-completion surveys

These surveys are completed by the targeted individual respondent, and are sent either via email or post. Increasingly web sites feature self-completion questionnaires, although the fact that respondents are on the web site in the first place and therefore self-selecting limits the value of the response.

This type of questionnaire is the cheapest to administer, as it does not involve the employment of an interviewer, either on the phone or face to face. However, it is also the least likely to be completed so has the lowest response rate. Individuals are much less likely to complete a lengthy questionnaire, so the most effective self-completion questionnaires are those that require "tick box" answers. The other danger of a low response rate is that the end result can be based on an unrepresentative sample.

Surveys via interview

These can be face to face or over the telephone, structured, semi-structured, or unstructured.

Structured surveys are fully constrained by the requirements of the questionnaire and are usually of a tick box nature.

Semi-structured surveys use a questionnaire, which has a combination of tick box and open-ended questions, allowing a degree of probing by the interviewer.

Unstructured interviews are used to provide qualitative data, and the interviewer usually just has a list of topics to introduce to the discussion.

Surveys by interview have a higher response rate than postal or email interviews, and face-to-face interviews generally have a slightly better response rate than telephone interviews. The telephone is quicker and more economical, but there is a danger that in some cases it is unrepresentative, as individuals with ex-directory numbers cannot be included.

Focus groups

These also produce valuable qualitative data, and are useful in that they provide the opportunity for individual's comments to "spark off" ideas and discussion from the other members of the group. The group is usually made up of 8-10 members. The value of the data depends on the selection of the respondents and the competence of the group "moderator", who needs to be carefully trained.

Observation

This is a technique increasingly used in retail environments, particularly to look at shopping behaviour and thereby inform category management. Video cameras are often used, although "headcounts" are carried out by personal observers. This can be relatively expensive, but reports on shopping behaviour can be jointly commissioned, sharing costs.

Experimentation

Test marketing is the most obvious form of experimentation, where for example, a mini-launch of a new product might take place in a smaller, similar market to the intended whole. This allows the customer response to the product and its promotion to be considered, without the risk/cost of a full launch.

Simulations and laboratory tests are also forms of experimentation.

Activity 9.1

Taking a research objective from the work place, design a project using a number of different primary and secondary methods of research, giving reasons why each method is appropriate.

Primary research in action

There are several Case Study examples in the main text for this module that clearly demonstrate primary research in action. Although primary data is more expensive to collect than secondary data, it is essential in exploring customer tastes, attitudes, and changes in lifestyle, in a way that informs a specific industry, organisation or product/service range.

Primary research can play a role in investigations in many sectors. For example, the Audit Commission carried out national research on childbirth and audited the maternity services provided by the National Health Service (NHS) Trusts in England and Wales. As part of this research they contacted a random sample of new mothers to get a "users" view of the service provided.

Research company SRG in the USA conducted research on behalf of a client who was looking to launch an online lifestyle management portal, targeting the over 50s. SRG conducted a three-phased research study:

- Secondary research to explore potential competitors and partners.

- In-depth interviews to confirm initial concepts, develop potential alternatives, and assess consumer demand.

- Focus groups of consumers who are Internet users and members of potential partner organisations.

To see yet another example of primary research in action, visit www.rajar.co.uk (Radio Joint Audience Research Limited), set up to provide a single measurement of radio usage in the UK. The organisation uses a combination of a personalised diary, completed by the listener, with an interview with one member of the household.

As a final example of the use of primary research, let's look at advertising research. It is essential that the target market for a particular product or service "like" the advertisement that is used to promote it. "Likeability" is one of the key factors that define whether or not a potential customer intends to buy the product, so it is therefore a key promotional objective.

Liking an advert does not necessarily mean that it promotes positive emotions, as consumers will say that they like an ad that they remember because it put across a powerful, relevant message. The advertiser wants to create empathy with the target market, so the message should be relevant and meaningful or of value to the individuals in that target market.

So, after the target market has been defined, how does the agency or the company devising the promotional campaign ensure that its' advertising is "likeable"?

Communications research is essential. Pre-tests are often carried out through focus groups to evaluate the impact of various message concepts before the final campaign is put together. These produce qualitative data that can be used to inform the final ad that is produced.

Following the campaign, measurements can be made through coupon returns or the level of enquiries received, if these have been the campaign objectives. Surveys might be used to assess any increase in brand awareness or to assess the level of attitude change effected by the campaign.

Post-tests also include recognition and recall tests, which can produce quantitative data about whether a particular ad is memorable to the appropriate target market, and which of a group of ads is recalled most readily.

There has been much press coverage recently of the inadequacy of marketers looking to target the over 55 age group, as their ads have frequently been patronising and unsuitable. Pre- and post-testing would be particularly useful techniques for these "grey marketers", who appear to be targeting their messages inappropriately, with detrimental results.

Secondary research in action

We have already covered the sources of secondary data in the previous Session, as well as looking at some of its uses. Let's look at an example of secondary research in action.

A mobile phone company is looking to develop a new package for its customers. Issues for consideration include both primary and secondary research.

1. **The need that the package satisfies**

   Qualitative consumer research will confirm what the target market wants and is willing to pay for. Focus groups can be relatively inexpensive to set up, but need to be managed well. They can also be time consuming to carry out. However, they are valuable in ensuring that the company is following the right track. It would be all too easy to make the assumption that a reduction in charges is what customers want and then find out that what they really want is a higher standard of service or a better international network for example (primary research).

2. **Competitor products**

   The company needs to check that none of its competitors are going as far as it is in the development of such a package, so it can retain a competitive edge by being "first" to market with its offer (secondary and primary research).

3. **Price thresholds and impact on profit margins**

   Would the planned pricing structure be at a level where sufficient sales could be generated to satisfy all stakeholders? The City and shareholders of the company need to be satisfied, but so do potential and existing customers (primary and secondary research).

4. **Likely improvement in market penetration**

   How long will the particular market exist before it reaches saturation point? Analysis of trends (secondary research).

5. How the market is growing

What is the overall size of the market? What proportion of it do they hold? How would the launch of this new package change their market share? (secondary research).

Items 3-5 involve quantitative data, some of which will be available internally, and some from secondary sources. Manipulation of this data, taking into account the findings of the qualitative research, will shape the overall package launched.

Finally, if we consider how research can be used to develop customer relationships, the first stage of research often involves the analysis of internal records to identify customer groups with which the organisation wants to establish relationships (secondary research). The second stage is then to establish whether customers want or need to establish relationships with the supplier. For example, in commodity markets, where products are difficult to differentiate, there may be no point in trying to establish relationships (primary research).

Activity 9.2

You have been supplied with the following data on the proposed introduction of two new customer services.

New Customer Service Activity	Estimated Cost	Expected Return
Telephone Helpline	$20,000 per annum	50% of the total cost is expected to be recouped through an arrangement with the company's telecom service provider.
Online Internet Support	$10,000 per annum	This is expected to be self funding by selling advertising space on the web site.

Write a memo to the Customer Services Manager that covers the following points:

1. Given that you can only recommend one of the above to be introduced in the current financial period, explain which one you would choose, justifying your recommendation.

2. Discuss further data you would like to obtain before confirming your recommendation and briefly comment upon how and where you would obtain the necessary data.

Case Study

Stress-free shopping

FACTFILE

Company: Tesco Plc
Company Name: Tesco.com
Brand name: www.Tesco.com
Original date of national launch: 1996
Market category: Retail (e-commerce)

Tesco.com rapidly established itself as both a leading player in UK e-commerce and the world's most popular online grocery service. Launched in 1996, by August 2000 Tesco.com was available to 91% of the UK population.

According to Nielsen/Net Ratings, by November 2000 the number of people online in the UK had reached 19.98 million. Today, that figure is estimated to be over 22 million. Recent research by AOL Europe/Roper Starch concludes that 55% of UK online consumers regularly shop online, and reports from Datamonitor indicate that Britain is the biggest market for online grocery shopping.

The online sector accounts for 0.4% of the UK grocery market, with £408 million worth of groceries purchased through the Internet last year. More than half that figure was spent at Tesco.com, which currently has a 53% share of the online grocery market. 'Our strategy in launching Tesco.com was obviously to grow the overall business, not to cannibalise it', says Head of Marketing, David Clements. 'The established Tesco brand values... were already in place by association. We positioned Tesco.com as "a convenient way to shop."'

The web site is just another channel to market, but because it is not constrained by bricks and mortar it can deliver a far bigger range than stores. 'Many of our top stores for example, will carry the Top 50 CDs. Tesco.com can offer every CD currently available in the UK.' Clements says.

Research is key. Every store undertakes customer satisfaction surveys on a regular basis via telephone or email. Question times are held and Clubcard data is analysed. 'We know from this that 74% of our shoppers are ABC1s, with the less price-sensitive ABs accounting for over 50%. Between 70-80% are female, with convenience clearly being the key factor in their decision to shop online.'

In 2000, Tesco.com's marketing spend was £10 million. The promotional campaign focused on dramatising Tesco's tag line, "Every Little Helps", and tying www.Tesco.com into the company's overall messaging. Press and TV ads highlighted the convenience of shopping online. Widespread brand awareness was achieved via a number of targeted marketing initiatives, involving what Clements describes as "comparatively little" marketing spend. These included the use of the existing store network to promote the online service by point of sale advertising, which allowed Tesco to reach the 12 million people who pass through its stores each week.

'Welcome packs and targeted HTML emails to Tesco.com customers also proved highly successful, resulting in a 10-30% response rate throughout the year. We additionally established affiliate deals with major portals based on cost-per-click or cost-per-sale,' Clements says. The Tesco Clubcard magazine, mailed to over 6 million customers, was used as a vehicle for a range of promotions, while PR activity focused on national, consumer and vertical media. In November 2000, a Press Watch report placed Tesco in the number two position in terms of UK press coverage, with Tesco.com cited as a major contributor to its overall press coverage.

Measuring effectiveness

With the number of registered customers now well in excess of 1 million, Tesco.com has been recognised by research companies Datamonitor and Gomez as the world's leading online grocery service. Not only does the service attract a lot of new customers from Tesco's competitors (10% of customers who have switched claim that it is as a result of Tesco.com), but 30% of the online customers shop nowhere else on the web.

At £10 per customer, the cost of acquisition is low compared to companies such as Amazon.co.uk, who cite a figure of between £50-£100. In 2000, Tesco.com achieved its sales volume target, moving from £50 million in 1999/2000 to over £230 million in 2000/2001.

Tesco is also gaining market share in the non-food sector, and sales are growing rapidly in areas such as electricals, entertainment and clothing. Although Tesco.com made a loss for the full year in 2000 (due to investment in the non-food side of the business), 2001 saw the brand's run rate turn profitable.

Meanwhile, the launch of Tesco Access, a text based HTML service that allows customers to access the service from their TV sets and pocket PCs, emphasises the retailer's commitment to lead the market in technological innovation. The service also makes it easier for visually impaired customers to shop online.

By the end of last year, Tesco.com had extended its coverage to 95% of the UK population. Through joint ventures the Tesco.com model has been introduced internationally. The company is currently considering introducing its service to Korea, which has the highest Internet penetration in the world.

Source: *Marketing Business,* May 2002.

Questions

1. What are the main forms of primary research mentioned in the Case Study? What methods are used to collect the data?

2. Suggest further research that would be useful to Tesco in launching and maintaining their online service.

3. The Case Study mentions that Tesco analyse data that they obtain from their Clubcard. What advantages does this data offer them?

SUMMARY OF KEY POINTS

In this Session we have introduced the sources and uses of primary data and covered the following key points:

- Qualitative information explores attitudes, opinions and feelings.

- Quantitative information is expressed in numeric terms and can be measured more easily.

- Primary research methods include:
  - Interviews.
  - Focus group discussions.
  - Survey methods.
  - Observation.

- Many research projects include both primary and secondary information.

Improving and developing own learning

The following projects are designed to help you develop your knowledge and skills further, by carrying out some research yourself. Feedback is not provided for this type of learning because there are no "answers" to be found, but you may wish to discuss your findings with colleagues and fellow students.

Project A

Talk to colleagues in your Marketing Department about the ways in which the results of marketing research projects have benefited your business. Discuss the likely impact of not carrying out any research.

Project B

Find out how your organisation gathers data for its customer database. Could the method be improved?

Project C

Find out if your organisation records customer complaints. What analysis has been undertaken of such records? Has this been translated into any action?

Feedback to activities

Activity 9.1

The answer you give to this activity will vary depending on the project you chose. Check the primary and secondary research methods you selected against the content of the text to ensure that the methods are appropriate.

Activity 9.2

The activity asks for a memo, so your answer should be in a memo format.

a.   Key points you should have included are:

Telephone helpline

Positives:

- Offers personalised contact.
- Customers may find it easier to explain their problem to another person.
- Additional lines will speed up the service.

Negatives:

- No matter how many lines we have, people can take time to explain their problem, causing the lines to be jammed.
- The cost is higher and we only recover 50% of it.
- Human errors may occur.
- Line failure could badly disrupt the service.

Online service

Positives:

- Customers can obtain information from the web site on a number of issues.
- They can send in their queries 24/7, which we can retrieve when convenient, providing better support than if customers were to experience engaged phone lines.
- Company image will be improved – in touch with technology.
- By selling ad space we can generate profit from the site.
- Customer care costs could be cut.
- High numbers of customers can access at the same time.
- Can automate some responses, saving time and money.

Negatives:

- Some people will still prefer to speak to someone.
- Web site security can be an issue.
- Relies on customers being able to access the Internet.

I recommend the online service. However, please note the need for further information (below).

b. Information on competitor offerings – web sites, brochures, sales personnel feedback.

Research into customer perceptions of such changes – primary research.

Performance of our existing customer care system – internal records.

Session 10

Observing behaviour

Introduction

This Session looks at the use of observational research in making marketing decisions. As technology develops, there are more and more ways of gathering such data. Here we examine both mechanical and personal methods. In addition, the use of "mystery shopper" research is considered, both in terms of its advantages and its disadvantages.

LEARNING OUTCOMES

At the end of this Session you will be able to:

- Describe the various procedures for observing behaviour.
- Explain personal methods of observation.
- Explain the advantages and disadvantages of "mystery shopper" research.
- Explain mechanical methods of observation.

Observational research

Watching people buy products in supermarkets can provide valuable data about purchasing behaviour and shopping habits. For example, researchers might observe how long customers wait in line to be served at McDonald's restaurants at different times of the day, in order to assess the effectiveness of their fast food operations.

Videoing is a form of observation that can be used, but this form of data gathering can encourage bias, especially if the respondent is aware of the process.

Mechanical devices might also be used to support observation, such as cameras, recorders, counting machines, and equipment to record psychological changes. For example, a special camera could be used to record eye movements, to detect the sequence of reading advertisements and product packaging.

This method of data collection can be used to support other areas of study, as the results measure people's behaviour, although it doesn't measure people's feelings or opinions.

Uses of observational research

Market research is a systematic collection of information about markets, and the most commonly used methods of collecting that information are by interview – either in person, by telephone, or by self-completion questionnaire. However, in some situations the objective of the research is to record behaviour or other facts. This can be done either mechanically or in person.

One of the characteristics of observation as a means of collecting information is that there does not have to be deliberate participation on the part of respondents, so the information can be collected unobtrusively.

Essentially observation studies focus on non-verbal behaviour. Thus attitudes, expectations, motivations and intentions cannot be observed. What can be observed includes:

Behaviour or action	e.g. actual movement.
Spatial relations	e.g. location of items.
Verbal behaviour	e.g. announcements made, greetings offered.
Temporal behaviour	e.g. how long something takes.
Physical objects	e.g. items in stock in a shop.
Visual records	e.g. items included to illustrate a publication.
Expressive behaviour	e.g. facial expressions, tone of voice, body language.

Examples of mechanical observation include traffic counters, recording on camera purchaser behaviour in store, recording patterns of visits to an Internet site, or meters to record family television viewing patterns.

Personal observation is used when the object of observation is not predictable, routine or repetitive, or when there is some reliance on interaction (as in the case of mystery shopping). The information is collected by an individual (interviewer) and recorded on a form (questionnaire).

The point about using personal observation as a method of information collection for market research purposes is that the information to be collected has to be systematically identified, and the recording of events must also be systematic. It is not appropriate to just "see what happens" and record this in a haphazard way. The tasks, actions, objects or expectations of behaviour must be specified in advance and then recorded against that specification.

The observation may be of:

- Physical objects (such as the counting or recording of stock in a retail setting).

- Human behaviour (such as the standards of service in a restaurant).

- Content (such as the analysis of information content in competitor brochures).

One widely used application of personal observation is the use of "mystery shopping" in monitoring service standards in organisations. The interviewer plays the role of a customer or potential customer and follows specified actions while recording the response of the branch or organisation to actions or requests. Mystery shopping might be used to monitor whether a retailer is providing correct information to a shopper in a friendly manner and without a lengthy delay. The information collected should not be subjective, such as an opinion – 'I had to wait a long time to be served', but rather should use objective measures such as 'I was served in under 5 minutes', or 'I waited more than 10 minutes for someone to greet me'.

Instead of asking questions from a questionnaire, personal observation records against a pre-set specification – that specification being based on the research brief. This might for example be a list of brands you might expect to find in store, or the size and format of the product/packaging against which the interviewer must record the levels of stock and prices.

There are obviously some ethical issues associated with observation as a means of data collection. Reference should be made to the Code of Conduct of the Market Research Society which addresses issues such as the right to privacy and avoiding entrapment by misleading or lying.

Activity 10.1

Suggest six suitable uses for observation in market research studies.

Mystery shopping

Mystery shopping was once thought of as invasive because employees were not aware that they were being monitored, and were therefore unable to withdraw from the interview. However, over time it has become an acceptable practice because staff are told that they will be monitored from time to time. This type of research is used to assess the effectiveness and quality of service, especially where the interface with staff is complex.

In mystery shopping, the customer organisation meets with a research company and develops a questionnaire and scenario for the "mystery shoppers". The study is carried out in the customer store and a paper-based report is completed showing the results.

Studies can be carried out in the following ways:

Visits

A visit is made to a distribution outlet e.g. a shop, branch, store, by the researcher posing as a "real customer". The researcher monitors and gives feedback on the actions taken by staff by completing a questionnaire or short report.

Video

Video mystery shopping is where a researcher posing as a customer uses a hidden camera. A predetermined script will be used and then following the completion of the scenario the shopper evaluates the level of service and image of the store. A film is prepared and supplied as part of the report.

Telephone mystery shopping

By using trained call centre staff and/or external researchers posing as "real customers", calls are made to an organisation. These calls are tape-recorded. This is an ideal tool for staff training.

Internet

An Internet mystery shopping programme entails the researcher accessing the company's web site. The purpose could be to "assess" the web site in terms of:

- Ease of use.

- The visual impact on a typical member of the public.

- Whether the web site allows sales queries and transactions to be made online.

Activity 10.2

Talk to fellow students or marketing colleagues who have some involvement in mystery shopping programmes. List the benefits that such a programme can produce for an organisation, including the marketing department.

Case Study

Big brother is watching you

Ethnography is a term most of us associate with an anthropologist in a remote village studying the arcane rituals of a lost tribe. But the world is running out of lost tribes, and anthropologists are increasingly to be found "at home" studying the rituals of supermarket shopping, Saturday nights out, or mobile phone use.

These are no longer academic exercises but projects funded by major companies anxious for detailed insights into consumers, which are inaccessible through other methods. Rather than polling large samples or interrogating focus groups, ethnographic researchers enter the lives of a small number of subjects, living with them, following them around, observing and noting their behaviour.

By living with their subjects for a number of days, ethnographers are able to observe consumer behaviour at first hand and to participate in it, and thereby test their interpretations of behaviour directly with the participants.

In one example of a recent ethnographic project, researchers from Intel took the number 73 bus and watched how passengers used their mobile phones. In another example (the BT taxi project), a video camera was put in the back of a black cab to investigate users' attitudes towards citizenship and community. In the US, companies as varied as Hallmark Cards and Procter & Gamble have made ethnography an integral part of their understanding of their consumers.

Making sense of the data

'People have been calling stuff they do ethnography for a while, but now people are waking up to a demand for real ethnography,' says Simon Roberts of ethnographic research consultancy Ideas Bazaar. 'There's a distinction between those who claim to practise ethnography but have never studied it and have done no research, and those who do it and have studied it and know the literature,' he says. 'You've got to be trained in anthropology. You need to have gathered material. You have to be able to put aside your preconceived ideas of the world and look at people from their own perspective.'

Ethnographic research projects, or "encounters", can generate huge amounts of information in the form of field notes, case studies, diaries and videos. It is only by drawing on the techniques and literature of anthropology that ethnographers can make sense of this mass of data. 'When you look at the rituals of going out, there's an important point the next day where people try to piece together the events of the previous evening,' says Roberts. 'And there are many anthropological articles which have a lot to say about rituals and post-ritual reintegration.'

Flashes of insight

According to Roberts, the results of ethnographic encounters often arrive as flashes of insight rather than presenting themselves as generalised truths. As an example he says, 'What technology does to humans is not nearly as interesting as what people do to technology: that's an anthropological perspective. People are complex, and you need a technique which can get beneath that complexity and uncover some gems that can help us.'

Despite its current popularity, ethnography should not be seen as displacing traditional market research techniques. 'Ethnography is a wonderfully useful tool for a very special business need,' says Nick Jankel-Elliott of strategic brand consultancy Happy Dog. 'Clients are bored at the moment and it's a fun thing to do. But it cannot do everything and cannot replace other forms of market research.'

Challenging assumptions

Jankel-Elliott sees ethnography as helping to challenge assumptions clients hold about consumers and their products, while generating new insights that help develop new product ideas. This can then feed into the design of focus groups and mass sampling that will quantify the opportunity. 'Ethnography is not research per se: it's looking at what we don't know we don't know,' he says.

One example is looking at the use of TV and the Internet, not as isolated technologies but within the cultural context of the living room.

'We found kids who were not just watching one programme or even channel surfing, but watching two programmes simultaneously. At the same time they're on the mobile and playing a videogame.'

"Ethnographic nuggets" such as this can be used by clients such as Sky to inform the way they package content and sell advertising across platforms.

In another case, ethnographers found that people expected different levels of service according to the "cultural codes" of different retail environments. So what is appropriate in, say, an electronics retailer, may not be right at the vegetable stall of a supermarket: important news for companies such as Ads, which operates across both segments.

'You can only find that out by living with people and going shopping with them,' says Jankel-Elliott. 'Market research dehumanises people, fetishises them as "ABC1s". Ethnography brings the humanity of people more to life.'

Reality check

Ethnography can therefore be a powerful tool for bringing marketing professionals back in touch with reality. As an example, James Crabtree, who runs the PwC and Microsoft-sponsored iSociety project for the Work Foundation think tank, points out: 'There's a real disconnection between the people who sell technology and the people who make use of it.' Crabtree believes marketers spend a lot of time marketing to themselves, with the result that a lot of technology advertising is aimed at "square specs people" or "Shoreditch man" – the fast-moving media types who demand connectivity at all times.

'When it's not a complete myth, you're talking about a risibly small group of people,' he says. 'How many people in the UK actually use email at work? It's less than two out of ten. Half have never received or sent an SMS message.'

Cutting through the divide

Ethnography can help cut through this divide, which Crabtree characterises as 'marketers are from Venus, consumers are from Mars'.

'How do you explain the fact that my mum goes to a restaurant without her mobile phone, which I find totally inexplicable?' he asks. You need to find out how one thing people do interacts with everything else they do: you can't get that from a focus group, you have to hang out with them.'

This "deep hanging around" (a phrase coined by Intel researchers), was used in iSociety's own research into mobile phones. 'A key factor in mobile phone usage is money,' says Crabtree. 'The majority of people struggle every month to afford their mobile phone. You get the unemployed single mother using it as a sanction: if you don't behave I won't give you any money to top up your mobile. People won't go to the pub so they can top up their mobile phone. You might get that kind of insight from a focus group but you'd need a really good question. Ethnography is quicker and easier.'

Significant value

Although ethnography is often characterised as expensive, Crabtree believes it can offer very significant value.

He says: 'Ethnography is not seen as equal to the traditional focus group, but to my mind you get twice as much insight for half the price. You get cool insight, deep insight, but not necessarily quantitative or universal insight.'

Ethnography is also useful in getting the results of research to a wider audience. 'People use polls as a way of getting press coverage but it's just not interesting any more,' Crabtree adds. 'Ethnography makes our research project seem more interesting, but we're not doing it just to be hip. I'm going for the method that gives me the deeper insight.'

Source: *Marketing Business,* November/December 2002.

Questions

1. Ethnography/observation is put forward as an alternative to running focus groups. Compare the two methods, identifying the advantages observation might offer over focus groups.

2. Identify from the Case Study the key outputs that are generated through ethnographic "encounters" and suggest how each might be of value to a marketer.

3. Ethnographers in the Case Study 'took the number 73 bus and watched how passengers used their mobile phones'. How might marketers have used the results of such a survey?

SUMMARY OF KEY POINTS

In this Session we have introduced how to observe behaviour and covered the following key points:

- Observation measures behaviour, not reasons for the behaviour.
- Categories include:
  - Visible and hidden.
  - Mechanised and human.
  - Participant and non-participant.

- Mystery shopping measures service delivery, often in a retail environment. Working to a brief, researchers act as customers, aiming to be objective and collect facts. More than one visit may be required.

- Observation can be carried out mechanically through scanners, electronic TV viewing meters, Internet cookies, and security or CCTV cameras.

Improving and developing own learning

The following projects are designed to help you develop your knowledge and skills further, by carrying out some research yourself. Feedback is not provided for this type of learning because there are no "answers" to be found, but you may wish to discuss your findings with colleagues and fellow students.

Project A

Talk to colleagues in your Marketing Department and identify whether observation has ever been used as a form of research. If it has, what was the purpose? If not, try to identify whether it would be appropriate for your organisation or industry sector.

Project B

Carry out your own observation project, analysing pedestrian or road traffic in a particular area at two contrasting times of day (e.g. 7 a.m. and 2.30 p.m.).

How might this information be of use to a marketer:

a. Manufacturing cars?

b. Looking to locate a new retail outlet?

Project C

Look at the following web sites for information on mystery shopping.

www.macphersonmysteryshopping.org.uk

> www.mysteryshopping.co.uk
>
> Make a list of the ways in which mystery shopping could be used for your own organisation, or, if mystery shopping is not appropriate, list the ways in which it might be useful to a major bank.

Feedback to activities

Activity 10.1

There are many possible uses of observational research. Listed below are six you may have noted:

- To observe levels of service delivered.

- To observe point-of-sale displays.

- To observe TV viewing patterns in the home.

- To observe shopping behaviour.

- To observe brands or products owned.

- To observe foot/pedestrian traffic in a particular retail area.

Activity 10.2

Some benefits of a successful mystery shopping programme.

- Motivated staff.
- Consistent sales processes.
- Continuous improvement.
- Focused training programmes.
- Successful product launches.
- Increased sales.
- Improved customer satisfaction.

- A customer's perspective.
- Reduced costs.
- Aids innovation.
- Working more efficiently.
- Improves time management.
- Assists in meeting regulatory requirements.

Session 11

Qualitative and quantitative methods

Introduction

This Session looks at methods of collecting data – both qualitative and quantitative. It defines the difference between the two, and explores the various research methods available and their relative uses. It also recognises that many studies incorporate both quantitative and qualitative research.

LEARNING OUTCOMES

At the end of this Session you will be able to:

- Describe and compare the various methods for collecting qualitative data.

- Describe and compare the various methods for collecting quantitative data.

In Session 9 we defined qualitative and quantitative data as follows:

Qualitative information

This is information that cannot be measured or expressed in numeric terms. It is useful to the marketer as it often explores people's feelings and opinions.

Quantitative information

In contrast, this is information that can be measured and expressed in numeric terms. For example, the percentage market share held, the number of customers buying our product in a certain month, or the number of sales calls made in a week.

In this Session we will look at the ways in which both types of data can be collected.

Quantitative research

There are various methods of collecting quantitative data, including:

- **Surveys** – both interviewer and self-administered. These are used for many purposes. For example, a postal survey (i.e. self-administered) might be used to measure the level of customer satisfaction with a service on a regular basis.

- **Omnibus surveys** – a cheaper method of survey that involves combining several short question "sets", each asked on behalf of a different client. Again, these have multiple uses. For example a client might want a short usage and attitude survey, investigating how often people eat ready-meals and who they are bought for, e.g. family, individuals, couples, to entertain.

- **Hall tests** – so called because they often take place in church halls etc. These are popularly used in product testing for taste, smell, touch or experience.

- **Placement tests** – used where the research depends on product use to inform the data collected. For example, where you might need to gather opinion on the ease of use of a new style of washing machine over a period of time.

- **Simulated test markets** – carried out as a stage in the new product development process. It involves setting up a product launch on a much smaller scale than full commercialisation to try and minimise risk. It is important to select a region that is representative of the total market, and to use the actual packaging and promotion you plan to use for the full launch.

- **Panels** – this involves recruiting a representative sample of the target population to track data over a period of time. It is useful in assessing trends, as comparisons can be made. For example, families may be recruited to report on their supermarket shopping on a regular basis. What do they buy? Which brands? How much did they pay? How has this changed over time?

All of these types of research have strengths and weaknesses in terms of:

- Purpose.
- Cost.
- Speed of collection.
- Ease of analysis.

Considerable detail on each type is given in the recommended texts for this module.

Activity 11.1

You have been asked to lead a small team to assess the appropriateness of your current price structures. Write a memo to your Marketing Manager that:

1. Lists and explains four reasons for conducting price research.

> 2. Explains how to conduct this type of research.
>
> 3. Clearly identifies and describes where the required information might be obtained.

Qualitative research

Qualitative research is a means of finding out not simply what people do, but why they do it. This is often referred to as attitudinal research, analysing people's beliefs and motivations. What is it that people like or dislike about a product or advert? Why do they feel that way? What would they prefer?

Surveys usually target fewer people in qualitative research than in quantitative research because the main process is exploratory discussions rather than asking everybody the same questions. As qualitative research is mainly about opinions it is much harder to analyse. However, it provides a greater understanding of what people need, want, feel and care about, which is extremely valuable information in its own right.

Qualitative research can be used on its own where numbers are not required, or can be used in advance of a quantitative study. It can also be used alongside or after quantitative research to help explain the data.

Research of this sort is almost invariably done face to face. One of the best-known techniques is **focus groups** (also known as **group discussions**), where 8-10 relevant people are brought together for a couple of hours or half a day to discuss something – a new product, an ad campaign, or views about a proposed change. The respondents' different views and experiences combine to create a unique and useful conversation.

A professional researcher or a facilitator guides the group through a series of topics previously agreed between the client and the agency, but in a less structured way than would be the case with a quantitative questionnaire (the discussion is more free flowing). Sometimes important ideas may emerge from the discussions that the researchers had not thought of, and these can then be followed up and explored.

Online focus groups are now a common, cost-effective way of collecting views and responses, and can be drawn from across the globe. This form of research is either an online discussion group headed by a facilitator, or a "chat" room discussion, similarly managed. For the latter, questionnaires can be sent out to be answered in people's own time, and can act as a prompt for the "live chat" session.

Not all qualitative research is done with groups. Individual interviews, often known as **depth interviews**, are sometimes more appropriate for certain studies, such as the collection of case study material. These can also include consultation with experts, which may form part of the initial exploratory first phase of a project.

Activity 11.2

For an in-house marketing research training day with your team you have been asked to produce a handout that:

1. Explains the difference between qualitative and quantitative methods of marketing research.

2. Provides a list of clear examples of the different tools used to gather different types of marketing research.

3. Gives the advantages and disadvantages of each example listed in 2.

Sessions 8 to 11 have covered the various types of data available to researchers, and some of the methods that can be used to extract that data. When taking decisions about research we need to ask ourselves the following questions:

- Look at the objectives of the research – can these be met by secondary research? If so, how can it be obtained? Any objectives not met by secondary research need to be obtained through primary research.

- Are we looking for qualitative data, quantitative data, or both? If it is both, which do we need first?

- Which collection options will be best? Personal, telephone or self-completion?

- If personal, will it be on street, at home, in office, in hall? Or will it be focus group, brainstorming etc.?

- If self-complete, will it be by post, email, Internet, fax, magazine insert?

- Finally, will the interview be structured, semi-structured or unstructured?

Case Study

Research to support a business case for investment

A major provider of business information (which publishes logistics information in hard copy format on an annual basis), identified a possible opportunity to provide information to their target audience of retailers via the Internet.

In order to justify the required investment, the Board wanted to have some evidence to support the case for moving online. Research was required to test the product in concept form amongst the international retail community. The key objective of the research was to establish the likelihood of purchasing the online service at different pricing levels.

A programme of 200 telephone interviews was conducted, the majority (2/3) were clients for the current hard-copy publication, and the remainder were non-users. Interviews were distributed across different world regions to reflect the distribution of target retailers: Western Europe (50%), Asia Pacific (20%), Central & Eastern Europe (10%) and North America (20%).

To qualify for an interview the respondent had to have a need for the specific information to be provided, as part of their current job function or role.

Main findings:

- Just over half of respondents (61%) spontaneously replied that they did not have any problems with obtaining the type of information to be offered as part of the proposed service.

- Of those who did experience problems, 14% said it was due to 'information not being up to date or inaccurate', 6% said it was 'incomplete information', and 4% said the 'information arrived too late' to be of use.

- On average respondents look for this information about 10 times a week, or twice a day.

Concept statement:

'A major initiative is being planned to create a new web-database of logistics information. The logistics information will be fully up to date with the data being provided by the logistics companies themselves. This user-friendly database will be held online, with fast and secure access, and will be searchable by company or by location.'

- Just over half of respondents (53%) in a spontaneous response to the concept being read out said that they thought it 'sounds like a good/very good/great idea', followed by 'depends on the cost/on charging structure for multiple users' (14%) and whether the 'information will be updated/accurate' (10%).

- The interest in the concept was 9% extremely interested, 32% very interested, 33% fairly interested, 16% not very interested and 10% not at all interested.

- Highest interest overall was from respondents in the UK, followed by Central & Eastern Europe, with the least interested being the Asia Pacific region.

- Spontaneous reasons why **not** interested in the concept included 'no regular need for this type of information/of limited use' (42%), followed by 'already get this information from other sources' (21%), and 'depends on cost/its value for money' (15%).

- Respondents were asked for their likelihood to subscribe at three different prices (read out in rotated order), the three prices varied according to their user size category.

  - 80% of respondents would be interested in receiving more information about the concept.

- 52% of respondents were VP/Dept. Head or Manager, 7% President/Director, and 13% Assistant Manager/Supervisor. 65% of respondents were male.

- 85% have personal access to the Internet, and 99% have some access to the Internet.

Outcome

The Board were encouraged by the high level of interest in having more information in due course, and were gratified to hear that some 80% expressed some interest in the idea. However, they were concerned that more than half of respondents do not perceive any problems at present. If they do not have problems and are in effect satisfied with their existing arrangements, then there may be no demand for the newly proposed online product.

The Board have requested that some follow-up research should be conducted to confirm the wisdom of the proposed investment.

Source: this Case Study is fictitious.

Questions

1.   What type of follow-up research would you suggest and why?

2.   Explain and give an example of when qualitative research should precede a quantitative survey.

3.   Explain and give an example of when a qualitative survey might be undertaken following a quantitative survey.

SUMMARY OF KEY POINTS

In this Session we have introduced qualitative and quantitative methods and covered the following key points:

- Quantitative research produces data that can be analysed statistically.

- Quantitative research methods include:

  - Interviewer-led telephone and face-to-face surveys.

  - Self-administered surveys.

  - Omnibus surveys.

  - Hall tests.

  - Placement tests.

  - Panels.

- Qualitative research deals with data too difficult to quantify, such as opinions and judgements. It is a skilled process and can be time consuming.

- Qualitative research methods include:

  - Depth interviews.

  - Group discussions.

Improving and developing own learning

The following projects are designed to help you develop your knowledge and skills further, by carrying out some research yourself. Feedback is not provided for this type of learning because there are no "answers" to be found, but you may wish to discuss your findings with colleagues and fellow students.

Project A

Draw up a two-column table. In the first column show the research methods that have been used by your organisation in the last two years. In the other column list the areas in which they have been used and the decisions they have informed.

Project B

Talk to colleagues in your Marketing Department and identify examples of qualitative and quantitative research undertaken in the past two years. Compare the results with the objectives each set out to achieve. How do they differ?

Project C

Talk to colleagues in your Marketing Department and identify whether any email questionnaires have been used by your organisation. Were these quantitative or qualitative in their design? How successful were they in achieving their objectives and in terms of their response rates?

Feedback to activities

Activity 11.1

This activity asks for your response to be in a memo format.

1. Four reasons for conducting price research include:

   Check prices against those of competitors.
   Check customers' perception of prices.

Decide how to price a new product.

Decide how to price across a product range.

2 and 3. This part of the answer will vary depending on the organisational context you chose.

Competitor information can be gathered through competitors' web sites, by phoning as a potential customer, or through your company sales forces' market intelligence.

Primary research would be necessary to establish customers' perceptions of prices.

Records of costs, combined with buy-response surveys, would help establish the price for a new product.

Internal records could be analysed for profitability and sales volume by product to inform pricing decisions across a product range. Also comparisons could be made with competitors' pricing across their ranges, before making pricing decisions.

Activity 11.2

Your answer should be in a suitable style and format for your own team and should cover:

1. Qualitative methods

Used to understand attitudes and motivations in purchase behaviour. Requires interaction between respondent and interviewer, and may be conducted via interviews or focus groups. Interviewers need to be well trained to avoid bias.

Quantitative methods

Often tick-box responses. Results can be measured statistically.

2. Tools include:

Qualitative	Quantitative
Questionnaires – semi-structured. unstructured.	Questionnaires – structured.

Focus groups.

Depth interviews.

Experimentation.

Observation.

Experimentation.

EPOS data.

3.

Method	Advantage	Disadvantage
Questionnaire.	Can provide detailed information.	May be subject to interviewer bias.
Focus groups.	Variety of opinions offered.	Relies on expertise of moderator.
Depth interviews.	Lengthy discussion can give much information.	Expensive to carry out.
Experimentation.	Can avoid risk through test marketing on smaller scale.	Can be expensive.
Observation.	Simple to carry out.	Only tells you what, not why.
EPOS data.	Can help identify buying patterns.	Volume of information needs to be managed.

Session 12

Questionnaire design

Introduction

This Session discusses questionnaire design and explores the important issues of layout, question flow, and the selection of question type. It considers not only the design of questionnaires for use in face-to-face, telephone and postal situations, but also the design of discussion guides for focus group discussions.

LEARNING OUTCOMES

At the end of this Session you will be able to:

- Explain the principles of questionnaire construction.

- Give examples of the various question types to be used in surveys.

- Design a questionnaire to meet a project's research objectives.

- Design a discussion guide to meet a project's research objectives.

Designing questionnaires

Before designing a questionnaire it is important to know in what context it is to be used. It might be used in personal interviews over the phone, or in a focus group, face to face, or by post. All of these contexts will affect the way the questionnaire is designed. The length of the questionnaire will also vary according to the method used.

Constructing questionnaires follows these stages:

- Clarify objectives.
- Consider methodology.
- Identify likely respondent.
- Develop question topics.
- Select question and response formats.
- Select wording.
- Determine sequence.
- Design layout and appearance.

- Pilot test.
- Undertake survey.

Design is also influenced by how the information is to be collected. For example, this might be via personal interview, telephone (manual or Computer-Aided Telephone Interview (CATI)) or self-complete.

Respondents must be able to understand the questions, and be motivated to participate. Few people enjoy being asked questions and filling in forms so the process needs to be simple and the questionnaire kept as short as possible.

The main considerations are:

- Type of questionnaire required:
  - Structured.
  - Semi-structured.
  - Unstructured/Topic guide.

- Types of questions that will work best:
  - Behavioural.
  - Attitudinal.
  - Classification.

- Types of answer and how interpretation is affected:
  - Open ended.
  - Closed.

- Design features to consider:
  - Sequence.
  - Wording.
  - Layout.
  - Length.

- Application – how it will be used:
  - Self-complete.
  - Face to face.
  - Telephone.
  - Observation.

- Language:
  - What is the normal language of the target audience?
  - Simplicity.
  - Jargon.
  - Vocabulary.

The following guidelines will help you when constructing a questionnaire:

1. Avoid complex or ambiguous questions that might confuse or encourage bias.

2. Answers such as "poor" and "fair" are meaningless and need to be replaced with "yes" and "no" where possible, or at least by descriptions that rate likes or dislikes in a more objective way.

3. Questions should be structured in a logical manner so that respondents are working with streams of thought where possible.

4. Personal questions should be kept to the minimum and kept till last.

5. Leading questions such as 'you don't think....do you?' should not be used as they encourage bias.

6. Be specific and don't rely on people to remember TV programmes and adverts they saw a while back.

7. Don't use words with an emotional content such as "love", "anger", "disappoint", etc.

8. Instructions for completing the questionnaire and returning it to the sender must be clear.

9. The layout should be appealing to the eye and not appear too cluttered.

10. Use probes and prompts such as 'if you answered yes to question 5 please state where you...'

Open questions play a valuable part in survey techniques, but their ability to be analysed is complex, so they should be kept to a minimum and worded very carefully. The risk is that answers will be forced into categories where they don't belong.

Questionnaires should be piloted with a small number of participants first to test for any faults or ambiguities.

Activity 12.1

Design a short questionnaire for the work place to assess the views of your Manager and team about a current issue or change in policy.

When constructing the questionnaire for the target audience consider:

- Question topics.
- Question and response formats.
- Wording.
- Sequence.
- Design layout and appearance.
- Pilot test.
- Undertaking the survey.

Questions

For most research topics a variety of questions and techniques should be used to understand the full range of opinions on a subject. Using a mix of personal and concrete questions, as well as general and abstract ones, will help you get more accurate answers.

Good questionnaire design is very important. You should craft simple, straightforward, unambiguous questions, which both the interviewer and the respondent understand, and which do not irritate or bore either of them.

The art of wording and structuring a questionnaire is one of the core skills of a professional researcher. It requires a high degree of empathy with respondents, and some common sense on what the limits are with regard to length, timing and environmental factors.

Questionnaires can be used face to face, by post, on the Internet, or over the phone. As with interviews, the questions may be structured or unstructured. Each approach has its limitations and the researcher must decide which is the most appropriate to elicit the correct level of information.

Open-ended questions

In-depth information is best obtained through open-ended questions. Highly sensitive information can also be explored and non-verbal behaviours captured and analysed. If researchers are tasked with obtaining attitudinal research, then this type of questioning allows for beliefs and values to be expressed. Responses can be examined and coded and turned into closed questions during the analysis stage. However, the limitations are that respondents may not wish to explore sensitive issues, and it takes a lot of time to analyse open-ended questions. Open-ended questions are mostly used for qualitative research and unstructured questionnaires.

Closed questions

Using closed questions in a sequential, structured format can exert control. Questions are closed-ended or fixed; that is, subjects select one response from a pre-determined set of answers. Respondents may be asked yes or no questions, or some type of ranking may be asked for, e.g. rank your preference for your summer holiday destination out of the following choices. One common method is to scale your answers from agree to disagree on a scale of 1-10. This method hopes to illustrate individual likes and dislikes.

An example of a questionnaire

The questionnaire below was designed to gain feedback from a sales force, so that the company, Synax, could improve its motivation programmes for the forthcoming year. International travel programmes are used as a major motivator and the company asked the Travel and Meetings Company to undertake this survey to identify key criteria for choosing the destination and activities for the next motivation programme.

The questionnaire was piloted with a group of sales staff and then launched to the whole sales force at a company briefing. The questionnaires were returned to the researcher by post and analysed and presented to the company decision-makers.

Synax

This research survey gives you the opportunity to influence the design of forthcoming Synax incentive and motivation programmes; it's **your** chance to create the incentive that appeals to **you!** The information collected can be unattributed if preferred.

Thank you very much for taking the time to participate.

SECTION 1: PERSONAL DETAILS

1. Name: ....
   (You may remain anonymous if you wish)

2. In which region do you work?

❑ South West   ❑ London
❑ North West   ❑ Midlands
❑ North East   ❑ Other (specify below)

....

3. What position do you hold?

❑ Business Unit Manager
❑ Account Manager
❑ Account Executive
❑ Sales Support

4. Are you:

❑ Male   ❑ Female

5. What is your age?

❑ 18-25   ❑ 26-35
❑ 36-45   ❑ 46+

6. What professional qualifications have you attained?

....

....

....

....

7. Do you hold membership of any professional associations? If so, which?

....

....

....

8. What is your marital status?

❑ Married   ❑ Single

9. Do you have children?

   ❑ Yes   ❑ No

10. In what type of accommodation do you live?

    ❑ Flat   ❑ House
    ❑ Bungalow   ❑ Other (please specify)

    ....

    Is this accommodation:

    ❑ Rented   ❑ Owned

SECTION 2: LEISURE PURSUITS/LIFESTYLE

11. What are your 3 favourite pastimes when relaxing? Please rank the top 3 in order of preference (where 1 = 1st choice).

    Rank

    ❑ Taking the family out.
    ❑ Going to a movie.
    ❑ Going to a nightclub.
    ❑ Drinking at a pub or wine bar.
    ❑ Eating out with friends.
    ❑ Going to or giving a dinner party.
    ❑ Staying at home to watch TV.
    ❑ Participating in a sporting activity.

12. What are your hobbies?

    ....

    ....

    ....

13. What sporting activities do you enjoy?

    ....

    ....

    ....

14. From questions 11, 12 and 13 above, which is your favourite leisure activity?

   ....

   ....

15. What are your top 3 favourite films? Please rank in order of preference (where 1 = 1st choice).

   Rank

   1. ....
   2. ....
   3. ....

16. Which are your 3 favourite music albums? Please rank in order of preference (where 1 = 1st choice).

   Rank

   1. ....
      ....
   2. ....
      ....
   3. ....
      ....

17. Of those cultural activities you attend on a regular basis, which are your favourites? Please rank in order of preference (where 1 = 1st choice).

   Rank

   ❑ Art exhibitions.
   ❑ Ballet.
   ❑ Cinema.
   ❑ Concert, Classical.
   ❑ Concert, Rock/pop.
   ❑ Dance.
   ❑ Opera.
   ❑ Theatre.
   ❑ West End Musicals.
   ❑ Other (please specify).

   ....

18. If you were being treated to a night out, all expenses paid, which of the above cultural activities would you most like to attend?

....

....

SECTION 3: MOTIVATION/INCENTIVE PROGRAMMES

19. What type of incentives have you received in the last 2 years:

    a. As an individual.

....

....

....

....

    b. As a team.

....

....

....

....

    c. Incentives related to specific products.

....

....

....

....

20. Which top 3 incentives motivated you most and why?

....

....

....

....

21. What, if anything, did you find demotivating about the incentives?

....

....

....

....

22. Which 3 methods of internal marketing have been most effective in motivating you to strive to win the incentives? Please rank in order of motivation (where 1 = 1st choice).

Rank

❏   Launch of the programme.
❏   Promotional merchandise.
❏   Letters of encouragement.
❏   Achievable targets.
❏   Timeframe for achievement.

22a. If you answered yes to 'timeframe for achievement', what is your preference?

❏   3 months   ❏   6 months   ❏   12 months

23. Please can you tell us which of the following rewards would motivate you to achieve business targets? Please rank the top 3 in each section (where 1 = 1st choice).

    a. Individual targets.

Rank

- ❑ Health farm/Spa voucher.
- ❑ Holiday abroad.
- ❑ Holiday abroad with spouse.
- ❑ Merchandise, e.g. electronic goods.
- ❑ Vouchers.
- ❑ Weekend break.
- ❑ Commission.
- ❑ Recognition through status.
- ❑ Other (please specify).

....

    b. Team targets.

Rank

- ❑ Group travel incentive.
- ❑ Away days.
- ❑ Company dinners with senior management.
- ❑ Public recognition for achievement.
- ❑ Outward bound programmes.
- ❑ Commission.
- ❑ Recognition through status.
- ❑ Other (please specify).

....

    c. Product targets.

Rank

- ❑ Training.
- ❑ Vouchers.
- ❑ Merchandise, e.g. electronic goods.
- ❑ Travel incentive.

❏ Prizes/Competitions.
❏ Commission margins.
❏ Other (please specify).

....

24. At what times of the year do you feel the least motivated?

❏ After Christmas.
❏ Spring.
❏ Summer.
❏ Autumn.
❏ Before Christmas.

SECTION 4: TRAVEL INCENTIVES

25. Which are your 3 favourite travel incentives of those you have attended in the last 2 years? Please rank in order of preference (where 1 = 1st choice).

Rank

1. ....

....

....

2. ....

....

....

3. ....

....

....

26. Which 3 factors motivated you the most about these travel incentives? Please rank your answer from 1 to 3 (where 1 = most motivational).

   Rank

   - ❏ Location.
   - ❏ Activity programme.
   - ❏ Accommodation.
   - ❏ Target audience.
   - ❏ Adventure element.
   - ❏ Weather.
   - ❏ Other (please specify).

   ....

27. What was the most demotivating aspect of these trips and why?

   ....

   ....

   ....

   ....

28. Please tell us which 3 destinations you would most like to visit if money was no object. Please rank your preferences (where 1 = 1st choice).

Rank	Long haul
❏	Australia.
❏	New Zealand.
❏	Hong Kong.
❏	Thailand.
❏	New York.
❏	Los Angeles.
❏	New Orleans.
❏	Singapore.
❏	South Africa.
❏	Canada.

Rank	Short haul
❑	Paris.
❑	Madrid.
❑	Amsterdam.
❑	Rome.
❑	Tenerife/Canaries.
❑	Turkey.
❑	Cyprus.
❑	Dubai.
❑	Malta.
❑	Portugal.

29. Please tell us briefly what attracts you to these destinations.

....

....

....

....

30. If you had £1,000 to spend on luxury goods for your trip, which 3 items are you most likely to purchase (giving brand names if known).

1. ....

....

2. ....

....

3. ....

....

31. When and where was your last family holiday?

....

....

....

32. When and where was your last single holiday?

....

....

....

SECTION 5: ADDITIONAL INFORMATION

33. Can you suggest any different approaches to target sales activity?

    a. Individual targets.

    ....

    ....

    ....

    ....

    b. Team targets.

    ....

    ....

    ....

    ....

    c. Product targets.

    ....

    ....

    ....

    ....

Thank you for your co-operation.

Types of questionnaire

As previously mentioned, there are three main types of questionnaire used in market research.

A structured questionnaire is typically used for quantitative research. They may be self-complete or administered by an interviewer, either face to face or by telephone. Question areas are well defined and the questions are always asked in the same words and sequence. Some or most of the answers can be anticipated, and the answers are recorded on the questionnaire, often by ticking boxes or circling appropriate answers.

A semi-structured questionnaire uses a combination of open-ended and closed questions, and may be used for qualitative and/or quantitative research. They are conducted either face to face or by telephone. The interviewer may use some prompts or probe for further information, and the answers are normally recorded on the questionnaire.

An unstructured questionnaire is sometimes termed a discussion guide or topic guide, and is most frequently used for focus groups or for "depth interviews". The discussion guide is in essence a checklist for a well-qualified and trained interviewer to use to elicit the desired information. The answers may be recorded in written format, or tape/video recorded with transcripts subsequently produced.

Designing a discussion guide

A discussion guide is used to steer the course of a discussion, whilst allowing the respondent(s) a free rein in their answers. The person conducting the interview is known as the moderator for a focus group, or the interviewer for a depth interview.

Clearly the discussion guide cannot anticipate all the questions in advance and needs to be flexible enough to accommodate unforeseen avenues of discussion. The whole point of a depth interview, whether one-to-one or in a group, is that it should be flexible and dynamic. Each question asked depends on the content of the previous answers (and also on the moderator's perceived meaning of those answers).

Because a part of the content is dependent on the type of respondent and what they have to say, no two interviews or discussions are likely to follow the same topic order or content. Typically it is an adaptive process, whereby the moderator learns from each new interview/discussion.

The guidelines for good questionnaire design also apply to developing a discussion guide. These include:

- Focus on the specific objectives.

- Consider the respondent – their interest, ability, language (terminology).

- Pay attention to sequence, wording and length.

In addition, the discussion guide can include a variety of stimulus material and projective techniques, designed to generate ideas and response.

Stimulus materials include actual products, literature, advertising or promotional material that can prompt discussion or reaction to a client's product or those of their competitors. Additional material might include concept boards, mock-ups or word boards.

Projective techniques might include word association, sentence completion, cartoon completion, obituaries, personification or role playing.

The key decision in designing a discussion guide is the 'what should be asked' decision. Other aspects, such as phrasing, sequence or layout, which are critical to questionnaires, are of subsidiary importance in a discussion guide.

One method of designing a discussion guide is to start by assuming a length of discussion (typically one to one and a half hours). This needs to be borne in mind when devising the content of the discussion, so that it is not overly ambitious in the number of topics it can cover. As a general guideline, you can cover a maximum of 6 to 8 themes within an hour and a half focus group. This allows roughly 10 minutes per topic – more for some and less for others.

Next, decide on the topics to be explored and the "props" (the stimulus materials or materials for projective techniques).

For each topic, decide on a list of possible question areas to cover when discussing that topic and the prompts that could be used. The questions are not used in a formal way, but represent ideas to keep the conversation going, or to steer it on course so that one comment doesn't lead other participants off on an irrelevant tangent.

The opening topic should normally relate to the participants, their background and experience, if relevant to the discussion of course. For example, if it were a survey on DIY, you might ask about the type of residence – whether house or flat, old or new, owned or rented. This opening topic is meant not only to "set the scene", but to help the participants feel more at ease with one another.

The topics generally are drawn directly from the research brief. Typical topics include:

- Introductions.

- Products currently used.

- Brands known and used; likes and dislikes in general of the product.

- Spontaneous reaction to client product/advertising etc.

- Likes and dislikes of the proposed product.

- Suggested improvements.

- How well the product/ad/message meets expectations.

- Overall conclusions – a summing up of the views expressed, with direct reference to the key objectives of the survey.

The biggest challenge in designing a discussion guide is to be realistic about the amount of information sought, whilst including in the topic guide sufficient content to ensure that the conversation keeps going and stays on track (in relation to the information specified in the research brief).

Activity 12.2

Choosing any product/service/industry you like, design a discussion guide to explore the likely reaction to a new product or service, and advise the client of the preferred option and optimal content.

Case Study

Cromwell's Breads Ltd.

Background

Mike Cromwell is the Marketing Manager of Cromwell's Breads Ltd., a medium sized regional bakery in Shropshire that was established in 1938 by Mike's grandfather, Tom. The company bakes and sells a number of well-known brands of bread under licensing arrangements, as well as its own label products. For the last 30 years, since Tom retired, the firm has been run by Sam Cromwell, Mike's father. It sells to retail shops, restaurants and institutions (schools, hospitals etc.).

Mike has been involved in the bread business all his life. As a boy he cleaned up at the bakery, and then later worked as a van driver/salesman during college holidays. After gaining his qualification in marketing, Mike began to work full-time for the company. After a couple of years in the office, his father appointed him Retail Sales Manager in charge of 24 drivers/salesmen. A year later he was put in charge of retail and commercial accounts and took the title Marketing Manager.

The problem

About three years ago Cromwell's Breads introduced a speciality line called Cromwell's Health Bread. Speciality bread is made from special or mixed grain flour and is heavier than regular bread. Not only have speciality breads been a rapidly growing segment of the bread market, they are also higher gross margin products. Industry trade publications identified the speciality bread consumer as coming from upper-income households and more highly educated than the typical bread consumer.

Mike knew that Cromwell's speciality breads were high quality and that they should be selling well, however the sales figures indicated otherwise. Cromwell's Health Line seemed to be rapidly losing market share to the national brands, whilst it was clear that the major supermarket chains such as Sainsbury's and Tesco's were selling a lot of their own-label speciality breads. Cromwell's salespeople could offer no real insight into why their Health Line was doing so badly.

Mike decided to do something that he had never tried at Cromwell's Breads Ltd. before – marketing research. He knew he would have trouble selling the idea to his father, but he also knew that he needed more information. Taking out a pad of paper, Mike began making notes on what he would like to know about the position of Cromwell's Health Line. Except for his own sales records and reports in trade publications, he decided he knew very little.

He was unaware of the growth rate of the speciality bread market in his area. He had no idea who bought his bread or his competitors, or how much consumers bought and how often. He didn't know who in the household asked for speciality bread or selected the brand. Another point that troubled him was not knowing the relative awareness of Cromwell's Health and its image among consumers. Finally, he hadn't been on a delivery route for some time and he thought he should get a better idea of retailers' attitudes towards Cromwell's Health Line.

Source: this Case Study is fictitious.

Questions

1. Design a short questionnaire to use to assess prompted awareness of Cromwell's Bread in face-to-face street interviews outside supermarkets, before undertaking an advertising campaign.

2. Design a short questionnaire to use as an alternative to the above to assess unprompted awareness of Cromwell's Bread in face-to-face interviews outside supermarkets in Shropshire and Yorkshire.

3. Design a discussion guide for a focus group to explore the main influences in the family buying unit as to what sort of bread is purchased and what brand is bought.

SUMMARY OF KEY POINTS

In this Session we have introduced questionnaire design and covered the following key points:

- Constructing questionnaires follows these stages:
  - Clarify objectives.
  - Consider methodology.
  - Identify likely respondent.
  - Develop question topics.
  - Select question and response formats.
  - Select wording.
  - Determine sequence.
  - Design layout and appearance.
  - Pilot test.

- Undertake survey.

■ Key aspects of design are spacing, quality of production, variety and coding/analysis requirements (covered in Session 14).

■ Question types include open-ended, closed and scalar (using a scale).

■ Focus groups/discussion groups require the design of a discussion guide for the facilitator.

Improving and developing own learning

The following projects are designed to help you develop your knowledge and skills further, by carrying out some research yourself. Feedback is not provided for this type of learning because there are no "answers" to be found, but you may wish to discuss your findings with colleagues and fellow students.

Project A

Gather examples of questionnaires from magazines, direct mail, reception areas, etc. Classify the types of questions in each. Now review online questionnaires. How do they differ?

Project B

Look at examples of questionnaires that have been used by your organisation. Could the questions used or the flow of questions be improved? Suggest improvements that could be made?

Project C

Some focus groups are observed through two-way mirrors. Talk to colleagues in your Marketing Department or at the agency that conducts your research, and ask if you can look in on a focus/discussion group, making notes about what you observe. Remember that during this exercise you are subject to the legal and ethical constraints represented by the Code of Conduct relating to the situation.

Feedback to activities

Activity 12.1

Your answer to this activity will vary according to the current issue or change in policy you selected. You should consider whether the responses are to be attributed to individuals or whether they should remain anonymous. A more honest response may be more forthcoming if arrangements are made to collate the responses independently of the organisation, so as to reassure employees that there will be no repercussions from the questionnaire.

The activity asks you to design a questionnaire to "assess the views" of your Manager and team, so you are looking for their opinions and attitudes. Qualitative, open-ended questions would therefore be particularly useful in this instance. Open questions need to prompt opinion and views to encourage people to say what they think or feel. However, the interpretation of these is much more complex.

For ease of analysis you may therefore have asked the following closed questions.

On a scale of 1-10 (with 10 being the highest rating), how would you rate the "ease of use" of the new IT system?

Have you seen an improvement in data-entry times since the new IT system was introduced?   Yes   No   Don't know

Consider the impact of the installation of the new IT system on your work. Listed below are pairs of statements that describe its potential impact. Mark an X between the two statements in a position that best reflects your view of the new system.

Easier to use	❑	❑	❑	❑	❑	❑	❑	More difficult to use
Time saving	❑	❑	❑	❑	❑	❑	❑	Time consuming
Modern	❑	❑	❑	❑	❑	❑	❑	Old-fashioned

Consider the training you received on the new IT system. Listed below are pairs of statements that describe the training you received. Mark an X between the two statements in a position that best reflects your view of the training.

Very useful	❑	❑	❑	❑	❑	❑	❑	Of little use
Easy to understand	❑	❑	❑	❑	❑	❑	❑	Difficult to understand
In-depth	❑	❑	❑	❑	❑	❑	❑	Too short

Activity 12.2

Let's suppose the brief relates to the packaging design of a beverage product. A possible discussion guide might look as follows:

Discussion on packaging

Introductions

Tell me a bit about yourself and your background.
What is your family unit?
Are you in paid employment or not?
Do you have your "meal occasions" together or as individuals?
Where do you shop for groceries? Why there?

Own-label products and packaging

Do you buy own label products?
Which products?
Why/Why not?
What is distinct about own label/those products?
Is the product different?
Is the packaging different?
What do you think of the packaging?
How could the packaging be made more interesting?

Packaging of coffees

Look at these coffees (present the group with various coffee packaging).

Which are unappealing? Why?
Which are a bit more appealing? Why?
What do you think of the (old) own-label/supermarket packaging?
What do you think of the new own-label/supermarket packaging?

New packs

What is your initial, instinctive reaction to the new packs at first sight (not detailed consideration)?

Consider the new packs as a group (NB: Props – can we produce eight to a page, colour, at least four copies to hand to participants?).

Do you like the colours?
Do you like the logo?
Do you like the descriptions?
Do you like the illustrations?
Any general comments?

Compare with other coffees

How does the new supermarket own-label packaging look against other brands?
Is it fun?
Does it appeal?

Patterns of use

What is your typical, daily pattern of coffee drinking?
Which type of coffee did you buy last? What brand was it? Where did you buy it?
Why that brand?
Which type of coffee do you prefer (beans, ground, granules, powder)? When do
you use the different types? Why?
On which occasions do you use/serve coffee? Breakfast? Mid a.m.? Lunch?
Afternoon? Dinner? Drop in? Coffee morning? Dinner party?
When having a cup of coffee out, what type of coffee do you have?
What is your experience of "coffee houses" like Costa, Aroma, Starbucks,
Whittards, etc.?

Awareness of types

Are you loyal to one type of coffee or do you experiment with different types of
coffee?
Which "types" do you know?
From which countries does coffee come from?
What might you expect of coffee from the following countries?

French	Italian
Brazil	Kenya
Colombia	Costa Rica

What words would you use to describe coffee (unprompted first)?
What do you generally associate with each country?
What would you expect of the coffee from each?

Now look at each illustration in turn (NB: Props).

Is it well communicated?
Is it fun?
Does it have good illustrations?
Is the colour appropriate?
Does it have good descriptions?
Do the characters and photos sum up the image of the coffee?

Associations

Again, what words might you use to describe coffee (NB: Props – have flip chart ready)?

What about:

Strong	Intense	Rich	Full-bodied	Sensuous
Nutty	Gentle	Lively	Fruity	Smooth

Overall reaction

General likes and dislikes.
Which packs are preferred? Why?

Session 13

Sampling

Introduction

This Session looks at the important topic of sampling. It explains the reasons why sampling is used and goes on to consider various sampling methods. It also explores the difficulties involved in selecting a suitable sample on which to base marketing decisions.

LEARNING OUTCOMES

At the end of this Session you will be able to:

- Explain the theory of sampling.

- Explain the potential difficulties of sample selection.

- Describe the various methods of sampling and explain when each is appropriate.

Sampling

It is not always possible for research to be carried out targeting the whole "population" (a "population" is a group of people the researcher wants to investigate, say people who buy ice cream), as it is rarely cost effective. In most cases the high cost of contacting everyone in a relevant population cannot be justified by the results or profits generated by doing so. A more affordable and popular option is therefore to obtain a representative sample of the population. However, it is important that the sample of the population taken is as accurate as possible, otherwise the results will be unrepresentative and unreliable for basing decisions upon.

It is important to remember that:

- Typically the sample is drawn from a population of relevance to the research e.g. the population of users of a particular product or population of suppliers of specific components etc.

- A sample is a limited number taken from a large group for testing and analysis, on the assumption that the sample is representative of the whole group.

- Samples are used to make an estimate of what the whole population of interest is like, what it thinks, or what it does.

The following provides a brief overview of sampling, as this is fully covered in the core text for this module. The process of sampling involves the following stages:

1. **Define the population** – this should have been defined by the objectives of the research.

2. **Define a frame for that population** – essential for probability sampling (defined below). The sample frame is a relevant list drawn from the population, from which the researcher will later select who is to take part in the survey.

3. **Select a sampling unit** – individual, family or company.

4. **Choose a method for selection of the sample** (probability or non-probability – defined below).

5. **Decide the sample size** – this will depend on the degree of accuracy needed and the amount of budget available.

6. **Define the sampling plan** – this adds a final degree of detail to the plan, and answers question such as: How do we define the head of the household? Is it the male or the highest income earner? What happens if a respondent decides not to finish the survey and leaves halfway through?

7. **Select the sample** – put the plan into action.

Definitions of different techniques:

Probability sampling

Sampling techniques include simple random samples, stratified random samples, cluster samples and multi-stage samples.

Non-probability sampling

This type of sample is chosen by the researcher for a specific purpose. However, there is a risk of a higher level of bias. Techniques include convenience sampling, purposive sampling, quota sampling, judgement sampling and snowball (where additional respondents are added following referral by original respondents).

Sample selection

Some managers continue to make important decisions without any research about the marketplace – the lucky ones are successful for a while. Other managers want endless research and statistics before making a decision – described as "analysis paralysis". Somewhere between the two is a balanced view.

One problem is how certain do you need to be that you have accurately forecasted the outcome of any action? For example, launching new products is a big risk unless you are sure that your new product will appeal to and satisfy the desires of your target segment. You would want a high degree of certainty that your new product does indeed appeal to the target segment before deciding to launch it. There are no absolutes, no guarantees, but the experience of the managers commissioning the research will help to create realistic boundaries and will, to some extent, help with the interpretation of the results.

Another question that needs to be asked is how large a sample do you need to be certain that the results are meaningful? If the investment is high, as would be the case if new capital equipment was required, or if a large advertising budget was being allocated, or if you were developing new channels of distribution, then you would need considerable reassurance that the results are indeed meaningful.

The analyst first needs to estimate what the whole population is. For example, say the research looked at a national sample of 1,000 people. Statistical theory shows that when a population is dominated by one or two mutually exclusive characteristics (e.g. red and white balls in a bag, or householders who have damp and those who don't – householders will either have damp or not, there is no third option, so it is mutually exclusive), we can set limits on the proportions of the total population with the same characteristic.

Let's take the example of households that suffer from damp. The table overleaf shows range of error estimates of percentages of population with one characteristic at 95% confidence levels (plus or minus) – for random samples.

Percentage	25	50	75	100	150	200	500	1,000
98 or 2	5.6	4.0	3.2	2.8	2.3	2.0	1.3	0.9
97 or 3	6.8	4.9	3.9	3.4	2.8	2.4	1.5	1.1
95 or 5	8.7	6.2	5.0	4.4	3.6	3.1	2.0	1.4
90 or 10	12.0	8.5	6.9	6.0	4.9	4.3	2.7	1.9
80 or 20	16.0	11.4	9.2	8.0	6.6	5.7	3.6	2.5
75 or 25	17.3	12.3	10.0	8.7	7.1	6.1	3.9	2.8
70 or 30	18.3	13.0	10.5	9.2	7.5	6.5	4.1	2.9
60 or 40	19.6	13.9	11.3	9.8	8.0	7.0	4.4	3.1
55 or 45	19.8	14.1	11.4	9.9	8.1	7.0	4.5	3.2
50	20.0	14.2	11.5	10.0	8.2	7.1	4.5	3.2

From the above sample we can see that because we have a sample of 1,000, and a figure of 2%, we can be reasonably sure that the total population of households contains no more than 2.9 (i.e. 2.0+0.9) per cent of households that suffer from damp, and the number will be no less than 1.1 (i.e. 2.0-0.9) per cent. The expression "reasonably certain" refers to samples of two mutually exclusive variables in a population with only those two variables. It means that 19 times out of 20 (or 95 times out of 100) the sample will indicate correctly that the characteristics of a total population lie between the limits indicated.

If a company selling damp materials believes that as a result of research they can predict a possible market penetration of 5% of the market (which using the above sample means between 4,000,000 and 150,000 customers), we see that this is not enough information to forecast adequately likely sales. This highlights the need to undertake further research, say with the retail sector, to give a further estimate of predicted sales.

The challenge is to establish upper and lower limits within which you can be reasonably sure that the results will reduce uncertainty and risk.

Activity 13.1

Your organisation is about to conduct some market research into consumer buying habits for the products/services your company sells. You have been asked to prepare a presentation for a meeting being held to discuss the available options. Your presentation should cover the following points:

1. The type of sample to be selected, with reasons for drawing a sample this way.

2. How the sample would be drawn.

Sampling techniques

Random sampling

One process for obtaining a sample of people is random sampling. In this context "random" had a very specific meaning. The names of potential respondents are selected at random, by taking for example every tenth or twentieth name from a list of all the relevant people. If we were carrying out a survey of the general public, the names would be taken from the Electoral Register, and as many of those people as possible would be interviewed. **Stratified sampling** clusters people into groups (e.g. by age or gender), and a random sample is then taken from each group. However, this is a relatively expensive approach to research, so the majority of surveys use quota sampling methods.

Quota sampling

This type of sampling involves interviewing certain types of people. If the people whose views you need are all under 50 years old, both male and female, and must have children aged under 11, then the interviewers will be asked to find and interview people who match this criteria. When they have finished interviewing, you will have a sample, a set of respondents, all of whom are under 50, half of whom are women, and all of whom have children under 11. It provides you with a cross-section of all the people you are interested in.

Activity 13.2

Explain the implications of the following money-saving tactics:

i)   Taking smaller samples.

ii) Taking part in omnibus surveys.

Case Study

To sponsor or not to sponsor?

Camberley Hotel Group runs a chain of hotels across the country, most of which have leisure services (such as swimming pools and health facilities) in their complexes. Most of their hotels are successful, but they have a few based in city centres that are currently underperforming. Camberley are now seeking to reposition these hotels, and are aiming to attract the affluent IT business community. This would link with the Group's move into the IT market that has just been completed with a well-publicised acquisition.

As part of its overall communications strategy, the Group is now considering whether to give significant financial support to a large travelling trade show that will take place in three of the city centres where it has hotels aimed at IT users (retailers, dealers, Value-Added Resellers (VARS), consultants and end users), who range from a few Original Equipment Manufacturers (OEMs) to a significant number of Small/Medium-sized Enterprises (SMEs).

The Group is very keen to link itself with this trade show, which has the makings of becoming a major attraction in the IT industry, and where they have been given first refusal on a sponsorship opportunity. The shows have just been run without a sponsor and were apparently fairly successful. A unique theme was used, which appears to have been very popular, and it is planned to use the same theme, updated as appropriate, for next year's shows. If the Group decides to sponsor the trade show, its involvement will also be covered in two trade show publications.

No formal research was carried out by the organisers last time, either with attendees or with the market in general, and before committing itself to this support Camberley intends to do some research.

The key objectives are to establish what the market thinks of the unique theme, and whether they are likely to attend next year's shows. Typical of the information required would be:

Did they like the shows?

Did they like the theme?

What benefits did they get from attending them?

Will they attend the shows next year or recommend them to others?

Camberley, working with their research agency, has decided on the following survey design:

1. Initial desk research, including checking results from other, similar exhibitions, relevant press comments, any relevant published research, etc.

2. Qualitative – interview with organisers.

3. Qualitative – expert opinion. Interviews with one or more selected senior journalists or editors who covered the events last year.

4. Qualitative – depth interviews via the telephone with a sample of exhibitors.

5. Quantitative – short telephone interviews with a sample of exhibitors.

6. Quantitative – short telephone interviews with a sample of attendees, with particular emphasis on seeking any changes in attitude in any of the company segments analysed after last year's exhibitions.

Names, addresses and telephone numbers of exhibitors and attendees are available from the organiser's files for the purposes of the sampling frame, and analysis of these files regarding last year's exhibitions reveal that overall there were:

- 240 exhibitors.

- 18,321 attendees from 10,781 different companies, in the following categories:
  - 987 dealers.
  - 1,072 software developer or support companies.
  - 2,410 architects and design consultants.
  - 2,094 VARs.
  - 2,220 retailers.
  - 1,998 business users.
  - Plus a further 566 "other" or not specified.

Assume a budget of no more than £4,000 for fieldwork (i.e. the interviewing) for items 4, 5 and 6 of the survey design.

For the purposes of this exercise, also assume that the interviews for item 4 will cost £30 each and the interviews for items 5 and 6 will cost £10 each.

Source: this Case Study is fictitious.

Question

Taking into account the intended survey design, the identified key target respondents, and the indicated budget (as set out in the Case Study), what would be your proposed sample sizes? What is your reasoning for how you would conduct the research for items 1-6 of the survey design?

SUMMARY OF KEY POINTS

In this Session we have introduced sampling and covered the following key points:

- The sampling process is as follows:
  - Define the population.
  - Determine whether to sample or census (collect data from every member of the population).
  - Select the sampling frame.
  - Choose the sampling method.
  - Determine the sample size.
  - Implement.
- Sampling methods include probability and non-probability.
- Probability:
  - Simple random.
  - Stratified random.
  - Cluster.

- Non-probability:
  - Convenience.
  - Judgement.
  - Quota.
  - Snowball.
- The sample size chosen depends on a number of factors.

Improving and developing own learning

The following projects are designed to help you develop your knowledge and skills further, by carrying out some research yourself. Feedback is not provided for this type of learning because there are no "answers" to be found, but you may wish to discuss your findings with colleagues and fellow students.

Project A

Talk to colleagues in your Marketing Department about research campaigns that have been undertaken to research the consumer market. How were the samples selected? What were the advantages and disadvantages of this method?

If you are not involved in the consumer market, ask your fellow students to share their experiences.

Project B

Talk to colleagues in your Marketing Department about research campaigns that have been undertaken to research the business-to-business market. How were the samples selected? What were the advantages and disadvantages of this method?

If you are not involved in the business-to-business market, ask your fellow students to share their experiences.

Project C

Look at www.rajar.co.uk and read about their sample selection methods.

Feedback to activities

Activity 13.1

Your answer should be in the format of a presentation, ideally in the form of slides and notes.

1. Available options:

    Existing customers – postal survey (random sample).
    Gives a broad spectrum of views without bias.

    Non-customers – street survey (quota sample).
    Gives impression of a general survey.

    Existing customers – telephone follow-up (quota sample).
    Can be categorised.

    Focus groups – (quota sample).
    Gives more in-depth information.

2. Random sample – drawn systematically from the database.
    Quota sample – existing customers (profiling of customers).
    Quota sample – non-customers (random until quota reached).

Activity 13.2

i)   Taking smaller samples, so long as they are more "in-depth", can still be effective. The danger is that by taking too small a sample you will not collect representative or reliable views.

ii) Taking part in omnibus surveys can save money, but can take more time. It can also mean a lower response rate, as omnibus surveys tend to be longer questionnaires, and therefore those responding may not be the audience we want to target.

Session 14

Analysis and reporting data

Introduction

This Session considers the techniques for analysing both qualitative and quantitative data. Having completed any analysis, it then needs reporting back to the company that commissioned the research, or the internal sponsor of the project. The Session therefore also briefly explores the various methods of reporting the research findings.

LEARNING OUTCOMES

At the end of this Session you will be able to:

■ Demonstrate an ability to use techniques for analysing quantitative data.

■ Demonstrate an ability to use techniques for analysing qualitative data.

■ Write a research report aimed at supporting marketing decisions.

Analysing quantitative data

One way in which quantitative data can be obtained is from structured questionnaires that are either self-completed or administered by an interviewer. These types of surveys are typically larger in scale than is the case with qualitative research projects.

Analysis can be defined as the application of reasoning to understand and interpret data that has been collected about a subject. The aim of the analysis is to combine the answers to make a meaningful summary of the results, and so transform the data into information that is suitable for decision making.

There are a number of stages to the analysis process:

Data preparation

This stage of the analysis involves editing and coding the data.

Editing

The questionnaires must be checked for any errors or omissions. Any substantial problems may result in a questionnaire being rejected. The editing may be done manually by reading through each questionnaire, or can be done mechanically after a data transfer, when any missing data or inconsistencies are identified.

Coding

Coding is used to facilitate analysis and usually involves allocating a numerical code to each response.

Where a questionnaire has been pre-coded, the code numbers are printed onto the questionnaire and the answers ringed accordingly. For open-ended questions, or where the answers could not be anticipated, then the main groups of answers are identified and each is allocated a code number, which then constitutes the code frame. The "groups of answers", or code frame, is typically constructed by listing and grouping the responses on a selection of questionnaires, say 10% of the total. An infrequent response is coded as "other". The code number is then written onto the questionnaire.

Data processing

At its simplest, where the number of questionnaires does not warrant the use of a computer (typically under 100 questionnaires), the analysis and processing of data can be done by hand. Simple counts are made of the answers and percentages calculated.

However, if for example you wanted to see which suppliers were being used in different regions, you would want to conduct a cross-analysis of the figures. Cross-analysis requires that the questionnaires are divided into separate piles and then counts done within each pile, which is likely to give you unrepresentative answers if you have only a small number of questionnaires to draw your data from.

Computers can be used to analyse data, but this requires the data to be entered via a keyboard onto the computer; a time consuming and costly business. Alternatively there is the Optical Mark Recognition (OMR) system. An OMR form can be used, and the completed questionnaire is then put into a scanner that reads the data and stores it electronically. There are a number of such software packages available for the market research industry. Two examples include SPSS from www.spss.com and SNAP from www.snapsurveys.com .

Sometimes "data specification" is necessary, and this involves telling the computer what to do with the data, such as doing counts or percentages, or carrying out statistical tests. A computer programme or software package carries out the processing.

The main output will be in the form of tables, or "tabs" as they are sometimes called. These typically show the number and percentage of respondents in the sample as a whole, and in various subgroups (as specified).

A simple count of answers by hand or by computer (without cross-tabulations) is known as a top-line result or a hole-count. Tabulations can provide a much more detailed analysis.

Statistical analysis

In their simplest form, statistics such as frequency, percentage, average and dispersion can be used to describe data, and these are the most widely used methods to analyse quantitative data.

When a sample is used rather than measuring the population as a whole, the statistics only give an approximation of the population statistics, within a given range (confidence limits). Significance tests can then be used to measure the significance of the difference between two means or between two percentages, and other tests can measure whether differences in cross-tabulated data are statistically significant.

There are a wide range of other statistical analysis methods which look at relationships between variables, and these can be used as a basis for identifying segments, predicting outcomes, and drawing conclusions. These include:

- Correlation analysis.
- Regression analysis.
- Multivariate analysis.
- Factor analysis.
- Cluster analysis.

These techniques allow the researcher to maximise the insight provided, by giving a much more detailed analysis of the quantitative data.

Tabulations

Tabulations, or tables, show the survey results, and cross-tabulations allow comparisons to be made between sub-samples, such as demographics, attitudes or behaviour.

Components include the:

Base – the group of people that were asked the question.
Row – the answers to the question.
Column – also known as the cross-break, or banner, or breaks – the subgroups that are to be compared.
Content – this can be in number and/or percentage form.

Presentation

The analysed data can then be presented in many different ways. Common forms are tables, bar charts and pie charts.

Activity 14.1

From the table overleaf showing the results of a survey, make statements about:

How many respondents there are?
Which vitamin has the highest level of awareness?
Which are the demographic variables?
What is the cell size relating to the age group 35-44?
Which age group shows the highest awareness of vitamin C?
Which group of respondents has the lowest awareness of vitamin E?

Base – All Women	TOTAL	Age					Social Class				TV Region								
		16-24	25-34	35-44	45-54	55+	AB	C1	C2	DE	London	Anglia	South	Wales/SW	Central	Lancs	NE	Yrks	Brdr/Scot
Weighted base	1,035	179	219	173	136	327	179	282	254	320	260	89	123	125	200	144	75	142	101
Sample size	1,031	138	257	209	149	278	171	258	259	343	240	87	112	131	203	145	78	150	104
Multivitamins	428 41%	76 42%	120 55%	79 46%	60 44%	93 29%	80 45%	132 47%	111 44%	106 33%	110 42%	35 40%	50 41%	50 40%	86 43%	67 47%	38 51%	65 46%	31 30%
Vitamin B Complex	239 23%	44 25%	60 27%	57 33%	42 31%	37 11%	57 32%	73 26%	59 23%	51 16%	58 22%	16 18%	39 32%	24 19%	45 23%	33 23%	19 25%	37 26%	17 17%
Vitamin C	413 40%	82 46%	106 49%	70 41%	62 45%	93 28%	91 51%	113 40%	97 38%	112 35%	101 39%	38 42%	51 42%	47 38%	88 44%	62 43%	33 45%	50 35%	34 34%
Vitamin E	237 23%	48 27%	62 28%	44 25%	32 23%	51 16%	54 30%	69 24%	63 25%	51 16%	60 23%	15 17%	36 30%	20 16%	57 29%	34 23%	19 25%	28 19%	13 13%
Other single vitamins	103 10%	19 11%	26 12%	16 9%	21 16%	20 6%	27 15%	29 10%	29 11%	24 6%	24 9%	8 9%	26 21%	13 10%	22 11%	9 6%	13 17%	20 14%	3 3%
Cod Liver Oil	357 34%	44 25%	66 30%	72 42%	51 37%	123 38%	65 36%	120 42%	85 34%	87 27%	99 38%	33 37%	47 38%	36 29%	74 37%	38 26%	26 35%	57 40%	26 26%
Garlic Oil	144 14%	19 11%	31 14%	26 15%	19 14%	49 15%	35 20%	39 14%	37 14%	33 10%	34 13%	10 11%	16 13%	20 16%	31 15%	19 13%	11 14%	21 15%	10 10%
Calcium	89 9%	18 10%	26 12%	15 9%	17 12%	13 4%	17 10%	29 10%	18 7%	26 8%	32 12%	6 7%	17 13%	10 8%	14 7%	12 8%	3 3%	13 9%	6 6%
GLA	3 0%	0 0%	1 0%	1 1%	1 1%	0 0%	0 0%	0 0%	1 1%	0 0%	0 0%	0 0%	0 0%	0 0%	2 1%	0 0%	1 1%	1 1%	0 0%
Anti oxidants	9 1%	3 1%	5 2%	2 1%	0 0%	0 0%	1 0%	6 2%	3 1%	0 0%	4 1%	1 1%	2 2%	1 1%	3 1%	1 1%	1 1%	1 1%	0 0%
Other supplements	247 24%	50 28%	61 28%	49 28%	38 28%	50 15%	60 34%	71 25%	58 23%	58 18%	51 20%	21 24%	28 23%	34 27%	40 20%	31 21%	28 37%	45 31%	21 21%

Analysing qualitative data

As stated earlier, analysis can be defined as the application of reasoning to understand and interpret data that has been collected about a subject.

Analysis may involve determining consistent patterns and summarising the appropriate details revealed in an investigation.

The appropriate technique for analysing data will be determined by:

i)   The management information requirements.
ii) The characteristics of the research design.
iii) The nature of the data collected.
iv) Statistical analysis, which can range from a frequency distribution to complex multivariate analysis such as multiple regression.

Since qualitative research focuses on understanding, rather than measuring, it is the nature and content of what is said that matters. The meaning, rather than the number of people that are saying it or the frequency with which it is said, that is important. The focus is on words and observations, descriptions, visuals and interpretations.

The data that is collected is raw, undigested, and largely meaningless until it is arranged in some way, or analysed to produce useful and usable information. The researcher may wish to do one or more of three main things with the data:

- Display the data.

- Summarise the data.

- Draw conclusions from the data.

Qualitative data does not lend itself well to being displayed – in either chart or table form. Occasionally lists may be produced from the information collected and these can be "displayed", but for the most part what is required is to summarise the data and draw conclusions.

While quantitative data is often analysed using computers, qualitative research is more of an ongoing process of developing ideas as the research progresses. In that sense it is less tangible than the "hard data" that emerges from quantitative studies.

In qualitative research what is needed is to identify patterns and significant events that contribute to the final picture.

In exploratory research the main objective is to look for patterns of attitudes and behaviour, and thus develop a picture of how a particular group or segment behaves. This may result in some hypotheses that can be quantified at a later date.

In diagnostic research you are looking to solve a problem or explain the reasons behind an event. This tends to be based on lateral thinking, or on intuitive insight, rather than on any mechanistic sorting of data. The analysis relies on identifying the significant elements within the data that could provide an explanation of an event.

Where research is being used for creative development, the aim is to get close enough to the respondent's thinking and attitudes to be able to replicate this to the client.

Unlike quantitative data, there is very little documented about analysing qualitative data, and few agreed principles or standards of practice.

Qualitative research is often in the form of transcripts from focus groups, from depth interviews, or semi-structured questionnaires that have many open-ended questions.

One suggested approach to analysing a transcript is to:

i)   Start by referring to the survey objectives.

ii) Take each heading or objective and read through each transcript identifying behaviour, attitudes, or opinions of significance under each heading or objective (you can then number the references accordingly).

iii) Highlight (with a marker pen) any appropriate verbatim comments or quotes that support a particular view.

iv) Identify the extent to which a particular view is held by all, most, or a minority of those questioned.

v)   Decide which to report as "typical" of the respondent group.

vi) Decide which others to report as variations in behaviour/attitude.

vii) Select the quotes that you will use to illustrate the findings of the report.

Where semi-structured questionnaires have been used, the approach is similar, but is facilitated by the fact that the findings are typically grouped under individual questions. Where there are more than a dozen questionnaires, the patterns will emerge more easily if a simple Excel spreadsheet is used to record types of answer before deciding on the statement to be made.

Activity 14.2

Write an example of a statement that might be made on the basis of qualitative data, and how such statement might read if quantitative analysis had been applied. For this activity you may wish to look at the feedback before attempting to do this yourself.

Compiling research reports

As with other formal reports, a final research report should include:

- Title page.
- Table of contents.
- Executive summary.
- Problem definition.
- Research method.
- Research findings.
- Conclusions and recommendations.
- Appendices.

Case Study

Leisure web site research

A leisure related web site is to be launched by summer, and those involved now wish to have some research that will assist them in developing the marketing strategy for the brand.

The main objectives of the research are:

- To obtain a reaction to the web site **concept**.

- To identify the potential **USP** for such a site.

- To test the reaction to the **editorial tone** of the proposed site.

- To confirm the **content** of the site.

- To check the initial user reaction and experience in relation to the **usability** of the site.

Since background quantitative research has already been carried out to identify the potential target audience for the web site and to evaluate the likely penetration of the target market, the proposed research is very much qualitative in nature, with the intention being to understand the expectations, needs and likely reaction of those likely to visit the site.

It is proposed to run a number of focus groups to reflect a variety of potential target audiences/users for the site. It should be stressed that whilst the intention is to highlight distinctions between types of user, the research cannot attempt to quantify the likely extent of any behaviour or reaction identified.

Composition of focus groups

There are a number of variables that are likely to influence the appeal and success of the web site among those interested in leisure activities. These include the following:

Commitment to activities	–	keen v occasional.
Level of support	–	participate regularly v follow on screen/ in media.
Internet familiarity	–	use leisure related sites regularly v web savvy, but not for leisure.
Location	–	North of England v South of England.
Income	–	ABC1 (higher income groups) v C2 D E.
Age	–	young (under 25s) v older (over 25s).
Sex	–	male v female.

Undoubtedly there may be other variables that will influence the likely reaction to the product concept, but the above are the main criteria by which the composition of the groups will be specified.

Source: this Case Study is fictitious.

Questions

1. What would you suggest as possible headings for reporting back on the above research?

2. What kind of evidence would provide convincing data for the client?

3. Would you describe the research as exploratory, explanatory or confirming a hypothesis?

SUMMARY OF KEY POINTS

In this Session we have introduced how to analyse and report data, and covered the following key points:

- Analysis of quantitative data involves coding, data entry, tabulation and statistical analysis.

- Methods of analysing quantitative data include – statistical significance and hypothesis testing, cross-analysis and multivariate data analysis.

- Analysis of qualitative data involves organising the data – either manually or by computer.

- Qualitative data can be analysed by the following methods – descriptive, content analysis or text analysis.

- The final research report includes:
  - Title page.
  - Table of contents.
  - Executive summary.
  - Problem definition.
  - Research method.
  - Research findings.
  - Conclusions and recommendations.
  - Appendices.

Improving and developing own learning

The following projects are designed to help you develop your knowledge and skills further, by carrying out some research yourself. Feedback is not provided for this type of learning because there are no "answers" to be found, but you may wish to discuss your findings with colleagues and fellow students.

Project A

Talk to colleagues in your Marketing Department and identify the quantitative analysis techniques that have been used internally. If all research has been undertaken externally, examine the reports and talk to the agency about the analytical methods they used.

Project B

Talk to colleagues in your Marketing Department and identify the qualitative analysis techniques that have been used internally. If all research has been undertaken externally, examine the reports and talk to the agency about the analytical methods they used.

Project C

Talk to colleagues in your Marketing Department and examine copies of the reports from previous research studies. What techniques have been used and why?

Feedback to activities

Activity 14.1

Question	Answer
How many respondents are there?	Looking top left: the sample size is 1,031 female respondents.

Which vitamin has the highest level of awareness?	Look down the left hand column: the one with the highest percentage is multivitamins at 41% awareness.
Which are the demographic variables?	Age and social class are the demographic variables used.
What is the cell size relating to the age group 35-44?	There were 209 in the sample in that age group.
Which age group show the highest awareness of vitamin C?	Look at the line with vitamin C. Look at the age bands. We see 25-34 has the highest percentage, with 49% naming it, compared with 40% in the sample as a whole, and only 28% in the 55+ age group.
Which group of respondents has the lowest awareness of vitamin E?	Looking across the line with vitamin E, it was named least often by those in the 55+ age group – only 16% compared with 23% in the overall sample.

Activity 14.2

Exploratory research can be used to identify the key decision makers in a buying decision. From this qualitative research it may emerge that "the normal pattern of behaviour" is that a team of people are involved. The research will help to identify those making the decision, although it could be that one key person has the final say.

After conducting depth interviews, you discover that this is indeed the case. In later research, you might seek to quantify in what percentage of cases the Design Engineer is involved in decisions, and in what percentage of cases the Purchasing Manager has a say. This would be quantitative research.

Qualitative statement

In a qualitative statement the findings might read:

In the majority of cases the decision to purchase is made by a team of people, including the Production Manager, the Purchasing Manager and the Design

195

Engineer. The research indicated that it is seldom the decision of a single individual. A typical comment was:

'We each have a say in the sourcing of that component. While Chris (the Purchasing Manager) ensures we have continuity of supply, I rely on Nick (the Design Engineer) to make sure the design is up to standard...'

Quantitative statement

In a quantitative statement the findings might read:

In 80 per cent of cases the decision to purchase is made by a management team. Where a team of people is involved, the Purchasing Manager is involved in 95 per cent of cases, the Design Engineer in 60 per cent of cases, and the Production Manager in 75 per cent of cases.

Session 15

Presenting the results

Introduction

In the last Session we briefly looked at reporting the results of major research projects in written format. This final Session looks at the ways in which the results of major research projects might be presented orally. It considers the skills of the professional presenter in putting together a structured presentation, designed to meet the needs of an audience. Finally, it explores the skill of making clear and confident recommendations for marketing and business decisions.

LEARNING OUTCOMES

At the end of this Session you will be able to:

- Plan and design an oral presentation of market research results.

- Use research and data to produce actionable recommendations for a marketing plan.

- Use research and data to produce actionable recommendations to support a business decision.

Presenting results

The first consideration when putting together recommendations is to review the objectives, and then interpret the findings in the light of these objectives. Tools that are useful for this include SWOT analysis, and also the implications of the findings for the 4Ps if you are developing marketing strategy.

Consider the following example of how to present results.

A research project was undertaken for an international signage company, looking at the opportunities for growth in the UK marketplace. The resulting information was specifically designed to illustrate the strategic options. A combination of findings and interpretation was presented to provide an overview of the possible strategic decisions.

Figure 15.1: Budget spend

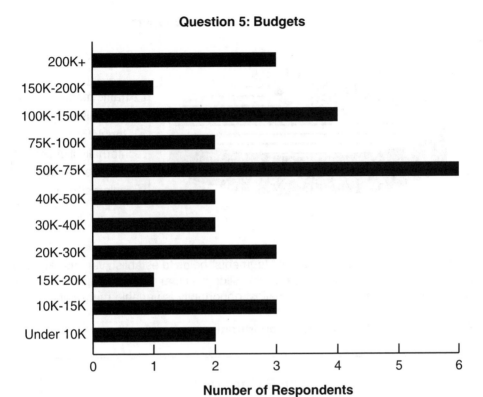

Question 5: Budgets

Using graphical explanations will help the viewer grasp the information much faster than if it is presented as a table. Graphs are particularly good for presenting quantitative data.

Figure 15.2: Opportunities for new schemes

Question 12: New Scheme Budgets

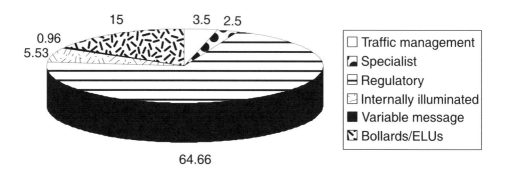

Using a pie chart to explain market "segments" helps to establish very quickly what the opportunities and threats are. In this slide it's clear that the major opportunity is regulatory schemes, and the smallest opportunity is variable messaging.

Figure 15.3: Top 3 geographic opportunities

> # Top 3 Geographic Opportunities
>
> - Lancashire CC £300,000 + Park and Ride, Town Centre re-signing, Bus Lanes, Traffic Calming and Car Parks.
>
> - Cardiff CC £250,000 + Town Centre re-signing.
>
> - Renfrewshire CC £70,000-£150,000 + Town Centre re-signing and Car Parks.

This slide shows that the data has been interpreted to show the key opportunities for new projects; extracted from tables within the report.

Figure 15.4: Acquisition opportunities

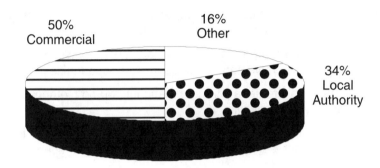

**Question 16: Providers of
New Road Traffic Signs**

50%
Commercial

16%
Other

34%
Local
Authority

The acquisition opportunities slide describes some of the strategic options from the findings, providing additional information to the other findings from the study.

It may not be part of the brief to interpret the findings, and an agency may just be asked to collect the data, leaving the commissioning organisation to make sense of it. However, most research companies will have access to specialised software to manipulate the data into probabilities, and are likely to be far more skilled at making judgements from the information collected.

Activity 15.1

Taking any information that is both qualitative and quantitative, develop a presentation for your Manager using graphical, pictorial and written slides. Also write some notes to accompany the presentation for clarification.

Reporting results

The information gained from the road signage research project was used to develop a marketing plan for the company over the next five years. The report covered the main findings of the survey, along with detailed statistics, narrative, and direct feedback from the project. The outcomes were then interpreted to make judgements about the opportunities and threats they faced.

Here is an example of how you can report results, in this instance showing the recommendations made from that study of the market share and growth potential in the road signage industry.

Strategic development

- Route Sign needs to develop strict geographic strategies, maximising its local relationships with key decision-makers and budget spenders.

- The sales team needs a programme of development activities to support better sales planning, to take advantage of these market opportunities.

- There is a need to create a stronger national "brand", emphasising size, breadth, capability and reliability.

- Total service packages, developing synergies such as temporary signage and other complementary services, would maximise budget spend from local councils.

- Networking and lobbying more senior decision-makers will assist in building the profile and strength of the Route Sign brand.

- A strategy needs to be developed to align the local sign shops.

Figure 15.5: Proposed Ansoff matrix – marketing strategy for Route Sign

Existing Product	New/Modified Products
• New road schemes e.g. Park and Ride. • Extend geographical coverage. • Partnerships/acquisitions.	• Microprismatic materials. • Total service provision (including maintenance). • Temporary signs.
New Markets	Diversification
• Private contracts. • Geographic segmentation by acquisition.	• New technology. • Commercial "off road" signing. • Civil contracting. • Vehicle graphics (mobile application).

The above options were presented in order of risk and investment requirements.

Existing products need to be marketed more aggressively and therefore sales training is an obvious remedy for improving sales revenue, as are marketing promotions.

New markets are necessary, and the lead-time would be at least a year whilst the necessary contacts are made and further research information sought.

New/Modified products require investment in tooling, staff, equipment and organisational change.

The highest risk strategy is diversification. However, acquisitions and mergers might be the most cost-effective way to approach new technology.

In this way the research company acts as a catalyst for change, supporting the decision making by making recommendations for the future. In some cases this level of consultancy is not required.

Meeting the client's needs

Studies have shown that much research that is commissioned is never used, because researchers fail to understand what the data will be used for. They must bear in mind that the findings should not be just technically competent, they should also support marketing decision-making.

The following points have proved to be particularly important in customer organisations:

1. Results conform to the client's prior beliefs.

2. The research is technically competent.

3. Presentation of the results is clear.

4. Findings are "politically" acceptable.

5. The status quo is not challenged.

Research may be ignored, even though it is perfectly valid, if it proves threatening to the organisation or the individual who commissioned the study. It can therefore be tempting to bias the results to achieve a desired outcome. Agencies recognise that giving the client bad news may well sour their relationship, but most researchers will be honest, and will abide by a code of ethics that recommends approaches to objective studies and interpretation of findings.

Product testing is an important part of commercial market research and can help meet clients' needs by helping them avoid costly mistakes. For example, in the 1960s the experts in corned beef knew for certain that the best product came form Latin America, but product tests showed that consumers preferred the less fatty African product. This was the start of the highly successful Fray Bentos special lean-cut brand.

New **product launches** often need research on several different elements of the marketing mix. Is the product concept right? Does the product work reliably? Is the packaging attractive? Are the brand associations right? Is the product experience right? Research agencies meet the clients' needs by developing comprehensive testing and modelling systems, as well as developing specialist techniques in **test marketing**.

In 1990 Barclaycard wanted to identify the affect of introducing a fee as a means of building profitability in a competitive market, and they needed to test how many customers they might loose, and which ones they might be. With the help of research four different packages were designed. AC Nielsen tested out a variety of different offers in promotional form using home interviews. The analysis covered the initial response to the options, discussions about the benefits, and the likely response. AC Nielsen then predicted the likely return on the planned promotion. The predicted results proved to be remarkably accurate, and played a crucial part in the new income stream (Research Works, 1991).

Presenting the results in person

Planning and preparing a presentation can be time consuming and nerve wracking.

The first stage is to work out what the objectives of the presentation are. Overall, these are to present the findings of the research. With this established, you then need to set specific objectives. To help you do this ask yourself:

- What do I need the audience to know?

- What do I want the audience to feel?

- What do I want the audience to think?

- What do I want the audience to do?

Presentation introduction and opening

First impressions are very important, so find out if you are to be introduced before you start to deliver your presentation. If so, then give the person introducing you a script. That way they will recognise who you are and will ensure that the audience knows what you are going to deliver. It is amazing how many people fail to give accurate introductions – after all it is not particularly important to them, but it is essential to you that you get off to the right start.

During the introduction to the presentation you **must** establish your credibility and tell the audience what's in it for them. Put yourself in their shoes. Let them know why they should give you some of their time.

It is also useful during the introduction to explain your approach, how long it will take, what breaks are planned, and when you would like questions. The introduction should prepare the audience, and the opening should provide you with the impact required to get the presentation off to a good start.

Effective openings include:

- Relevant or topical facts drawn from your presentation or other sources.

- Direct statements of fact and why they are important to the audience.

- Indirect statements that are of vital interest to the audience and linked to your outcomes – make that link.

- Vivid example to explain why the audience need to listen to your presentation.

Planning content and structure

If you wish people to remember you and respond to your presentation, then you must consider this when planning your content and structure. The content must be interesting, informative and **relevant** to the key issues. Information must flow logically so that people can follow your ideas easily.

Attention grabbers will be required, but do not fall into the trap of raising the level of excitement in the audience if it cannot be sustained at a reasonable level. It is more effective to maintain a steady delivery than put the audience through the ups and downs of a roller coaster ride – unless of course it is appropriate!

When planning content think about:

- Where you are going – take the audience on the shortest journey from the start to the finish of your presentation.

- Supporting your case with reasons, facts, figures, examples, references, etc.

- Using examples that will help the audience apply your ideas to their own situation.

- Delivering benefits, so that the audience is sold on your ideas, product etc. and want to know more.

Any idea that you want your audience to remember needs to be repeated (in one way or another) from three to ten times. When speaking to a large audience it is very difficult to observe how effectively individuals have understood, so it is important to reinforce your key points. You will not insult their intelligence if you do this in different ways.

Closing the presentation

It is important that you close positively but avoid hype and exaggeration. It is much more effective if you concentrate on the key issues and reinforce the message that you want the audience to go away with.

You will probably take questions at the end, even if you have been presenting to a small group who have chipped in informally to get answers at relevant points, so you may need to re-summarise, as the questions may have dislodged some of the key issues from the audience's mind!

Ensure that you have a strong close. Speak directly to the audience rather than relying on a list of bullet points on screen. This is when you must engage with the audience and ensure that everyone goes away discussing the key issues. Avoid abrupt endings – they unsettle and disrupt thinking patterns.

There are various ways of ending your presentation:

- Sum up then state your conclusion.

- Simplify a complex subject.

- Ask for action, making it easy for them to do what you want.

Supporting the presentation

Visual aids and other aids are used to:

- Appeal to different senses (acetates, music, demonstrations and sampling).

- Focus attention.

- Create a change of pace.

- Aid understanding.

- Create a more vivid and lasting impression than the speaker alone.

- Reinforce important points.

- Provide reference material for future use (handouts).

There are a number of ways of adding interest to your presentation.

Visual aids – acetates and PowerPoint

A word of warning. Avoid stunning graphic displays that reduce your presentation to a simple voice over! A picture can be worth a thousand words, but make sure it doesn't get in the way of you, the person, delivering the presentation. Remember to Keep It Short and Sweet (KISS).

Limit the number of bulleted list slides you use. The audience may be concentrating on one that is more interesting to them than the one you are talking about. Consider using slides that have no words on them at all.

When designing your visual aids, limit the number of points per slide, no more than six at most. Present figures as graphs and charts where possible.

Don't use your PowerPoint slides as prompts for your presentation or you will end up reading them out to the audience and then explaining each point. Very obvious and very boring.

Guide your audience where to look when you put up a visual aid. For example, 'If you look at the largest segment on the pie chart you can see that over 50%...'.

Do not turn to read from the screen. You will have lost eye contact with your audience and some people may find it difficult to hear what you are saying.

Using facts and figures

Use relevant facts and figures to back up your arguments and key points, but remember to identify the sources. Present figures in a table, in a chart, or as a graph for greater clarity, and draw people's attention to the specific information you want them to take away.

Simply presenting a chart that is obvious to you will not work. You must talk people through the information. Try to limit the number of segments in a pie chart or bars on a bar chart. Once you get over six it is difficult for people to decipher – particularly if they are sitting some distance away.

Delivering the presentation

When presenting, consider:

- **Smiling** – It releases a chemical in the brain that promotes a sense of well being and tends to be infectious. But avoid the Cheshire cat syndrome. Be natural. Be pleasant.

- Any idiosyncrasies that you have. For example, do you say "right" or "obviously" a lot or shift from foot to foot when speaking?

- Eye contact. Don't stare, but make sure you include everybody in the audience.

- Standing comfortably, but not too relaxed. Don't stand with your feet together because it may encourage you to rock from side to side. Stand firm with your feet slightly apart. Be confident and aware of the way you are communicating non-verbally!

- How you will overcome mistakes – we all make them! Don't apologise, just put it right and carry on confidently. If you are comfortable the audience will reflect this. If you get flustered or embarrassed so will they.

- Your appearance. Avoid flashy jewellery and clothes that rustle with every movement. Seek the advice of real friends and supportive colleagues if you are not sure what might be appropriate. Check clothes are clean and tidy with no missing buttons or frayed cuffs!

- Wearing comfortable clothes and shoes!

- Your gestures. Using your hands can be expressive, but waving your arms about is often very off-putting.

- Think of the audience as your friends and not the enemy – it will affect how you speak to them!

Vocal flexibility

Listen to effective presenters on television and radio and analyse why you find them interesting or pleasant to listen to. Do they:

- Use their voice expressively by varying tone?

- Vary the pace of delivery?

- Pause after important points and repeat if necessary?

In order to add meaning to what you say you need to use the right tone and body language. Look at these initially surprising statistics.

When we communicate the meaning of the message is relayed by:

7%	Content.
38%	Tone.
55%	Body language.

The receiver interprets the message using the above clues – each of which are open to interpretation and can easily be misunderstood. To stand most chance of getting the right message across, make sure that all three elements are consistent. If you want the audience to be happy then speak in a happy tone and use open body language.

Controlling a question and answer session

When taking questions:

- Believe that the person asking the question really wants to know the answer. It will make a difference to how you answer!

- **Listen actively** and answer the question asked. Don't try to take advantage of the questioner to get another point across.

- Seek clarification if you are unsure about what is being asked.

- Repeat the question if you are in front of a large audience.

- Be brief.

- If it is not of universal appeal then give a brief answer and get back to the questioner after the presentation.

- Respond to negatives – refer back to the facts in your presentation that support your position. Do not assume that the questioner heard these or realised their significance – they may have been distracted!

- If you cannot answer the question you may be able to ask someone else to take it, or promise to find out and tell the questioner when you will get back to them.

- Deal with irrelevant questions firmly but politely. 'If we had more time it would be useful to explore your point. Perhaps we can talk further after the event.' Don't waste other peoples' time.

Activity 15.2

Prepare guidelines for a new member of staff that outline the key points involved in making effective and interesting presentations.

Case Study

Presenting findings

The following represents the key findings and evaluation of a membership attitude and satisfaction survey for a membership organisation. Some small bits of information have been changed or deleted to protect the identity of the client company.

2.1 Key findings

1. The principal finding of the research was the extremely low profile of the organisation among the constituent member groups.

2. The majority of respondents know very little about the organisation, and hesitate to provide any description of what they do know the membership offers.

3. The number one reason to belong to the organisation is the default reason that one "has to" in order to take part in specific activities.

4. The organisation is perceived to be geared mainly towards one specific target group. As such it is considered to be of limited relevance to the average member.

5. All of the respondents would welcome closer contact with the organisation and would particularly welcome:

    - More information.
    - More focus on their type of member.
    - More general support.
    - More training courses.
    - More local activity.
    - More ideas.
    - More clarification.

6. There is little overt dissatisfaction with the organisation, and indeed many appreciate the extent of activity on what is assumed to be limited funding.

7. Members regret the extremely low profile of the organisation and recognise the potential to project a more attractive profile.

8. The majority of respondents were amazed to hear of the 15-20 services currently available to members and would welcome more information.

9. The services of greatest interest to members include…

10. There is a great deal of confusion about… service. As a result this is not generally perceived as a major benefit of organisation membership.

11. There appears to be some problem with membership records since many of those listed as no longer affiliated had presumed they were still members. There is very little deliberate discontinuation of membership.

12. Similarly, among those listed as no longer members, there was actually just one who had decided not to renew. Others did not renew as they were no longer active in this field.

13. The web site offers a great opportunity to communicate with members, but only if it is updated regularly and contains useful information.

14. The research indicated that there is a great deal of enthusiasm and commitment to the organisation among the various member groups, and there were many actionable suggestions that would result in a more supportive and satisfied membership.

2.2 Evaluation

The research highlighted a number of ways in which the organisation could meet the needs of their members and expand their reach by delivering services of interest to a wider membership. The recommendations which follow are based on the findings as revealed by the research. The agency has no detailed knowledge of the current policy and strategy being developed within the organisation, and these conclusions have not been discussed with the Executive. In the light of this, there may be parts of what follows which lie outside the bounds of existing thinking, and so the remainder of this section must be interpreted in the context of those considerations.

A marketing strategy is likely to deal with issues around the 4Ps as they are commonly labelled:

- Product.
- Price.
- Place.
- Promotion.

Some might also add a fifth 'P' of people.

In the context of the research objectives for the members' organisation the decisions to be made relate broadly to:

Product. How should one define the product i.e. the service to be offered to members? What should the positioning of that product be?

Price. To consider a review of the pricing structure as currently operated with varying categories of affiliation. To review also any additional potential revenue streams whether courses, merchandise or supporting materials.

Place. This normally relates to 'sales outlets or channels of distribution', but in the context of the membership organisation one could interpret it to mean the channel to market, in the sense of how the local committees and links might best be used as a channel to recruit members and/or to communicate with the target groups.

Promotion. The research suggested that this might be a number one priority for the organisation in terms of a deliberate strategy to raise the profile of their activity in general, and of the organisation in particular.

People. In this context the "people" element might represent both the people through whom the organisation works at a local level and also the potential membership.

Product

Some initial decisions must be made regarding the positioning of the organisation. These relate to:

a. **Who** is to be targeted? Whether the aim is to target only specific niche members or all potentially interested parties.

b. **What** is to be offered? Does the organisation want to be seen as mainly a regulatory Body upholding standards for key parties? Or will its aim be to penetrate to a more general participant' level and be more a central source of information and reference for all those with an interest?

c. **Why** should people join? Is the rationale for joining still to be the "necessity" of belonging? Or could one develop a prestige to belonging, such that people would want to be a member because there is kudos by association?

Once the positioning has been decided then the organisation will be in a position to determine exactly what the nature of the "belonging" represents, in terms of what is being offered to a potential member.

At present the range of offerings is so wide-reaching that none stand out as a "lead" proposition, and the low profile of the organisation means that members or potential members are not aware of what the potential benefits might be.

There are a number of ways the offering could be categorised, according to how the organisation plans to position itself. One possibility for example might be:

Core Products/Services	Information Services
Training and Support Material	Support and Development Activities
Commercial Services	Advice

Price

It was not within the remit of this piece of research to review the current pricing structure for the various levels of affiliation currently on offer. A more detailed analysis of revenue streams would be necessary in order to make any specific recommendations. The research suggested however that there could be scope to differentiate between those with a core interest in the activity and those with a peripheral interest. Some of the services listed above might be developed as profit-centres in their own right, which could be expected to cover their costs or even generate some net revenue, while others would be covered out of a central services fund.

Place

As mentioned earlier, what is considered under this heading is the channel to market, which currently appears to be primarily via local bodies. It is recognised that there is a limit to how much control the organisation can have over the local operations. However, it is not uncommon in commercial markets for independent "distributors" to develop their own sales strategies independently of the key "manufacturer". Nevertheless, it is appropriate for the organisation to set a certain number of Standard Operating Procedures to ensure that there is a greater consistency between local organisations. There are some examples of "Best Practice", and these should be shared widely so that others can gain ideas and converge over time to a better operating method. The research highlighted many examples of local organisations that had limited information about the central organisation. Clearly this layer should be a major priority in terms of future communication.

Promotion

One of the key findings of the research is the low profile of the organisation. There would be a greater appreciation of the organisation, and potentially a greater desire to join, if there was a greater awareness of the potential benefits.

It is evident from the research that there is substantial potential to make the target membership more aware of the organisation. Some consideration should be given to the ways in which the role of the organisation is highlighted in the context of building a general awareness of this business.

Once the positioning has been determined there are some natural activities that might be used to raise the profile. These include:

- Posters.
- PR activities.
- Open days.
- Seminars.

The research indicated that one of the reasons that members do not identify closely with the organisation is because they never hear from it. The maintenance and development of the database will be essential for future communications, and ultimately it could be a valuable asset in attracting sponsorship and in promoting the services offered by the organisation. With the growth in the use of email there is a relatively low cost option to keep in touch with the membership and to ensure they are kept informed of the most recent developments.

The research suggested that at present there is not a clear consistency in terms of communication with the membership – some receive a newsletter, others do not, some hear news via their local branch, whilst others have great difficulty locating such information. Some consideration should be given to the practicality of having brief telephone contact at least once a year with each member as part of a Customer Relationship Management (CRM) programme, which effectively could offer sales opportunities for value-added services offered by the organisation. At a minimum there should be some direct mail contact with the targeted individuals two to four times a year.

People

One of the dimensions highlighted by the research was the distinctions in expectations and needs between various categories of member. The "people" element highlights the diversity, and suggests the need to segment the market in terms of product/services, support, and communication. The communication "messages" need to be tailored to each audience. The main message is that there should not be a "one size fits all" approach to meeting member needs.

General

Although there are some policy decisions that will have an impact on future marketing strategy, the key to success will be to develop a communications strategy that takes account of the needs of the different segments as highlighted above. A part of the marketing strategy should be directed towards setting defined and measurable targets for each of the action points to be incorporated into the strategy. Depending on budgets, some consideration might be given to retaining the services of an external Public Relations Agency, to assist in achieving some of these targets relating to awareness of the organisation and of specific services on offer, as well as targets relating to raising the profile and achieving coverage of the organisation in local, regional and national media. As well as setting the targets, the marketing strategy would set realistic timescales for achieving such targets.

Source: this Case Study is fictitious, but is based upon an actual organisation.

Questions

1. Based on the details provided, what action points would you suggest?

2. How would you summarise the Strengths, Weaknesses, Opportunities and Threats facing the client (as revealed by the research)?

3. Draw up three slides for a presentation to summarise the findings and evaluation.

SUMMARY OF KEY POINTS

In this Session we have introduced how you can present results and covered the following key points:

■ Presenting market research results orally involves:

- Understanding your audience and responding to their needs.

- Structuring the presentation – introduction, methodology, key findings, conclusions and recommendations, and answering any questions.

- Delivering the presentation confidently and professionally.

- Presenting data appropriately using tables and charts.

■ There are common mistakes to be avoided, including:

- Assuming prior knowledge.

- Presenting for too long.

- Misleading information about accuracy or statistics.

- Distracting the audience from the key message through technology.

- Relying solely on technology that may fail on the day.

Improving and developing own learning

The following projects are designed to help you develop your knowledge and skills further, by carrying out some research yourself. Feedback is not provided for this type of learning because there are no "answers" to be found, but you may wish to discuss your findings with colleagues and fellow students.

Project A

Arrange with colleagues in your Marketing Department to attend a presentation made by your marketing research agency. Evaluate the presentation against criteria you develop. For example, how suitable was the language used for the audience? How well was the presentation structured? How appropriately were tables and charts used?

Project B

Put together a presentation for some secondary research you have carried out for your organisation. Make the presentation to a group of colleagues and ask for feedback on your presentation skills.

Project C

With a colleague discuss two business decisions, one that was a success and one that proved problematic. In what way would information have supported the decision making in the problematic business decision, and what lessons can you learn from the success story.

Feedback to activities

Activity 15.1

Your response to this activity will depend on the information you chose to present. Remember that it should be structured to meet the needs of your audience, and that you should make use of graphs and charts to put across quantitative findings.

Activity 15.2

Guidelines for making professional presentations

- Structure presentations using a beginning, main body, and summary/recommendations.
- Consider the audience to whom you are presenting.
- Set an appropriate objective and stick to it to give you focus.

- Keep the presentation short.
- Allow time for questions.
- Involve the audience when appropriate.
- Use charts and graphs to communicate complicated data.
- Be confident in the recommendations you make.
- Rehearse, rehearse, rehearse.
- Smile.

Glossary

The following relevant terms have been taken from the CIM's online glossary. If you would like to see a full listing of marketing terms please visit www.cim.co.uk, and look under Services and then the Library and Information Service section of the site.

Above-the-line – advertising for which a payment is made and for which a commission is paid to the advertising agency.

Account management – the process by which an agency or supplier manages the needs of a client.

ACORN (A Classification of Residential Neighbourhoods) – a database that divides up the entire population of the UK in terms of the housing in which they live.

Added value – the increase in worth of a product or service as a result of a particular activity. In the context of marketing this might be packaging or branding.

Advertising – promotion of a product, service or message by an identified sponsor using paid for media.

AIDA (Attention, Interest, Desire, Action) – a model describing the process that advertising or promotion is intended to initiate in the mind of a prospective customer.

Ansoff matrix – model relating marketing strategy to general strategic direction. It maps product/market strategies.

Balance sheet – one of the three parts of a financial statement showing the assets, liabilities and shareholders' funds of the company at a point in time, usually the end of the period on which the report is being made.

BCG (Boston Consulting Group) matrix – model for product portfolio analysis.

Below-the-line – non-media advertising or promotion when no commission has been paid to the advertising agency.

Brand – the set of physical attributes of a product or service, together with the beliefs and expectations surrounding it.

Break-even analysis – a technique used in decisions about cost, volumes and pricing of products and services. The break-even point is the point at which revenues based on a given price result in neither a profit nor a loss.

Budget – a plan in monetary terms of activities for a future period. Each department, function or unit in an organisation will usually have a budget against which its performance is measured. There are various forms of budget in organisations.

Business plan – a strategic document showing cash flow, forecasts and direction of a company.

Business strategy – the means by which a business works towards achieving its stated aims.

Business-to-business (b2b) – relating to the sale of a product for any use other than personal consumption.

Business-to-consumer (b2c) – relating to the sale of a product for personal consumption.

Buying behaviour – the process that buyers go through when deciding whether or not to purchase goods or services.

Cash flow statement – one of the three parts of a financial statement for a company, showing the main inflows and outflows of cash over a period.

Channels – the methods used by a company to communicate and interact with its customers.

Comparative advertising – advertising which compares a company's product with that of competing brands.

Competitive advantage – the product, proposition or benefit that puts a company ahead of its competitors.

Confusion marketing – controversial strategy of deliberately confusing the customer.

Consumer – individual who buys and uses a product or service.

Consumer behaviour – the buying habits and patterns of consumers in the acquisition and usage of products and services.

Contribution (also known as unit contribution) – it is revenue minus direct costs of production, promotion and delivery, and is usually expressed per unit. It is used to calculate break-even in cost-volume-profit analysis and pricing decisions.

Copyright – the law that protects the originator's material from unauthorised use, usually (in the UK) for seventy years after the originator's death.

Corporate identity – the character a company seeks to establish for itself in the mind of the public.

Corporate reputation – a complex mix of characteristics such as ethos, identity and image that go to make up a company's public personality.

Cost-volume-profit – a term describing the relationship between the three key variables modelled when determining the break-even point for a given price. Used during **pricing decisions**.

Costing – the process of determining costs and attributing them to the various activities undertaken in the organisation.

CRM (Customer Relationship Management) – the coherent management of contacts and interactions with customers.

Culture – a shared set of values, beliefs and traditions that influence prevailing behaviour within a country or organisation.

Customer – a person or company who purchases goods or services.

Customer loyalty – feelings or attitudes that incline a customer to return to a company, shop or outlet to purchase there again.

Customer satisfaction – the provision of goods or services which fulfil the customer's expectations in terms of quality and service, in relation to the price paid.

DAGMAR (Defining Advertising Goals for Measured Advertising Response) – a model for planning advertising in such a way that its success can be quantitatively monitored.

Data processing – the obtaining, recording and holding of information that can then be retrieved, used, disseminated or erased.

Data Protection Act – a law which makes organisations responsible for protecting the privacy of personal data.

Database marketing – whereby customer information stored in an electronic database is utilised for targeting marketing activities.

Decision-Making Unit (DMU) – the team of people in an organisation or family group who make the final buying decision.

Delphi technique – a forecasting technique in which the view or estimate of the future is compiled from inputs by a number of individuals, usually experts in their field, working independently of each other, usually in successive rounds.

Demographic data – information describing and segmenting a population in terms of age, sex, income and so on which can be used to target marketing campaigns.

Differentiation – ensuring that products and services have a unique element to allow them to stand out from the rest.

Direct mail – delivery of an advertising or promotional message to customers or potential customers by mail.

Direct marketing – all activities that make it possible to offer goods or services or to transmit other messages to a segment of the population by post, telephone, email or other direct means.

Direct Product Profitability (DPP) – the technique of using **contribution** to make decisions about price and monitoring performance of the organisation's assets, such as channels and production or retail space.

Direct Response Advertising – advertising incorporating a contact method such as a phone number or enquiry form with the intention of encouraging the recipient to respond directly to the advertiser.

Discounted Cash Flow (DCF) – a method, used in making **investment decisions**, for calculating the present value of capital expenditure and future revenues for a project based on a **discount rate**.

Discount rate – the rate used in **DCF, IRR** and **payback method** to discount future values to calculate the present value of an investment. It is either the interest rate or cost of capital.

Distribution (Place) – the process of getting the goods from the manufacturer or supplier to the user.

Diversification – an increase in the variety of goods and services produced by an organisation.

E-commerce – business conducted electronically.

E-marketing – marketing conducted electronically.

Electronic Point of Sale (EPOS) – a system whereby electronic tills are used to process customer transactions in a retail outlet.

Ethical marketing – marketing that takes account of the moral aspects of decisions.

Export marketing – the marketing of goods or services to overseas customers.

Field marketing – extending an organisation's marketing in the field through merchandising, product launches, training of retail staff, etc.

Financial statements – statements made by a company that present a "true and fair view" of its financial position at the end of a period, usually one year. They consist of a **profit and loss statement, balance sheet** and **cash flow statement**. Under company law in the UK, all companies are required to submit financial statements annually to Companies House; companies above a certain turnover have to submit accounts that have been independently audited.

Fixed costs – costs in an organisation that do not vary with the level of activity or sales. They are usually fixed over a certain period.

FMCG (Fast Moving Consumer Goods) – such as food and toiletries.

Focus groups – a tool for marketing research where small groups of participants take part in guided discussions on the topic being researched.

Forecasting – estimation of the probability and scope of future events and performance. A forecast is usually used as the basis for a budget.

Franchising – the selling of a licence by the owner (franchisor) to a third party (franchisee) permitting the sale of a product or service for a specified period.

Geo-demographics – a method of analysis combining geographic and demographic variables.

Grey market (silver market) – term used to define a population over a certain age (usually 65).

Industrial marketing (or business-to-business marketing) – the marketing of industrial products.

Innovation – development of new products, services or ways of working.

Internal customers – employees within an organisation viewed as "consumers" of a product or service provided by another part of the organisation.

Internal marketing – the process of eliciting support for a company and its activities among its own employees, in order to encourage them to promote its goals.

International marketing – the conduct and co-ordination of marketing activities in more than one country.

Internal Rate of Return (IRR) – a technique used in making **investment decisions** to determine the percentage rate at which the **Net Present Value** of an investment equals zero. In other words when the project breaks even, taking into account the time value of money. If the IRR is higher than the **discount rate** then the investment is worth considering; if it is less than the **discount rate**, the project will not break even.

Investment decisions – the decisions made in organisations by senior managers on investments in assets and capabilities of the organisation, based on the calculation of Net Present Value of capital expenditures and revenues.

Jury technique – a forecasting technique in which a group of people, usually experts in their field, work together to make a forecast.

Key Account Management (KAM) – account management as applied to a company's most valuable customers.

Logo – a graphic usually consisting of a symbol and or group of letters that identifies a company or brand.

Macro-environment – the external factors which affect companies' planning and performance, and which are beyond its control (SLEPT or PEST factors).

Margin – a generic term used to express profit as a percentage of sales. Gross margin is gross profit as a percentage of sales. Net margin is net profit as a percentage of sales.

Market development – the process of growing sales by offering existing products (or new versions of them) to new customer groups.

Market penetration – the attempt to grow ones business by obtaining a larger market share in an existing market.

Market research – the gathering and analysis of data relating to markets to inform decision making.

Marketing research – the gathering and analysis of data relating to marketing to inform decision making (includes product research, place research, pricing research, etc.).

Market segmentation – the division of the marketplace into distinct subgroups or segments, each characterised by particular tastes and requiring a specific marketing mix.

Market share – a company's sales of a given product or set of products to a given set of customers, expressed as a percentage of total sales of all such products to such customers.

Marketing audit – scrutiny of an organisation's existing marketing system to ascertain its strengths and weaknesses.

Marketing communications (Promotion) – all methods used by a firm to communicate with its customers and stakeholders.

Marketing information – any information used or required to support marketing decisions.

Marketing mix – the combination of marketing inputs that affect customer motivation and behaviour (7Ps – Product, Price, Promotion, Place, People, Process and Physical Evidence).

Marketing orientation – a business strategy whereby customers' needs and wants determine corporate direction.

Marketing planning – the selection and scheduling of activities to support the company's chosen marketing strategy or goals.

Marketing strategy – the broad methods chosen to achieve marketing objectives.

Micro-environment – the immediate context of a company's operations, including such elements as suppliers, customers and competitors.

Mission statement – a company's summary of its business philosophy, purpose and direction.

Model – simplified representation of a process, designed to aid understanding.

Net Present Value (NPV) – the value in today's terms of expenditures and revenues associated with a specific set of activities or project over a period of time, discounted at a specific rate. The main method for arriving at a NPV for a project is **discounted cash flow**.

New Product Development (NPD) – the creation of new products from evaluation of proposals through to launch.

Niche marketing – the marketing of a product to a small and well-defined segment of the marketplace.

Objectives – a company's defined and measurable aims or goals for a given period.

Packaging – material used to protect and promote goods.

Payback method – a method used in making investment decisions. Expressed as a point in time, it is the point at which a project breaks even. When it is used with a **discount rate** it takes into account the time value of money and is therefore more precise.

Personal selling – one-to-one communication between seller and prospective purchaser.

PIMS (Profit Impact of Marketing Strategies) – a US database supplying data such as environment, strategy, competition and internal data.

Porter's Five Forces – an analytic model developed by Michael E. Porter that analyses the competitive environment and industry structure.

Positioning – the creation of an image for a product or service in the minds of customers, both specifically to that item and in relation to competitive offerings.

Pricing decisions – decisions to determine the price at which products or services will be sold. There are a number of methods available to determine price taking into account the relevant costs.

Product Life Cycle (PLC) – a model describing the progress of a product from the inception of the idea, through its growth and maturity, to its eventual decline.

Profit – the amount that is left out of revenues at the end of a period once all the relevant costs have been deducted. Profit is measured at a number of levels, including gross profit (after direct costs), operating profit (after all operating expenses) and retained earnings (after interest, tax and dividends).

Profit & Loss (P&L) account – one of the three parts of the financial statement for a company, showing the revenues and costs over the period being reported.

Promotional mix – the components of an individual campaign which are likely to include advertising, personal selling, public relations, direct marketing, packaging and sales promotion.

Public Relations (PR) – the planned and sustained communication to promote mutual understanding between an organisation and its stakeholders.

Pull promotion – addresses the customer directly with a view to getting them to demand the product and hence "pull" it down through the distribution chain.

Push promotion – relies on the next link in the distribution chain, e.g. the wholesaler, to "push" out products to the customer.

Qualitative research – information that cannot be measured or expressed in numeric terms. It is useful to the marketer as it often explores people's feelings and opinions.

Quantitative research – information that can be measured in numeric terms and analysed statistically.

Ratio analysis – the use of financial ratios, usually as part of a wider analysis of an organisation and its current situation, to ascertain its performance and financial health. The analysis usually involves the use of profitability, liquidity, solvency, utilisation and investment ratios.

Reference group – a group with which the customer identifies in some way and whose opinions and experiences influence the customer's behaviour.

Relationship marketing – the strategy of establishing a relationship with a customer that continues well beyond the first purchase.

Return On Investment (ROI) – the value that an organisation derives from investing in a project.

Sales forecast – a forecast of the sales revenues expected for a future period. It is significant in that it determines the level of activity for the organisation for that period, and as such forms the basis for the other forecasts of costs generated by organisations. Considerable emphasis is therefore placed on its accuracy.

Sales promotion – a range of techniques used to increase sales in the short term.

Scenario planning – a technique used in planning to identify the possible future scenarios for an organisation, which can then be quantified and modelled and a view taken on the probability of the occurrence of each. This technique is particularly useful to organisations facing high uncertainty.

Sensitivity analysis – the modelling and assessment of the potential risks facing an organisation in a specific situation using the question "what if?". It is commonly used in planning at the forecasting stage, setting budgets and making investment decisions to take into account different circumstances and risks.

Skimming – setting the original price high in the early stages of the product life cycle to get as much profit as possible before prices are driven down by increasing competition.

SLEPT – a framework for viewing the macro-environment. Socio-cultural, Legal, Economic, Political and Technical factors.

SMART – a mnemonic referring to the need for objectives to be Specific, Measurable, Achievable, Relevant and Time-bound.

Sponsorship – specialised form of promotion where a company will help fund an event or support a business venture in return for publicity.

Stakeholder – an individual or group that affects or is affected by the organisation and its operations.

Supplier – an organisation or individual that supplies goods or services to a company.

Targeting – the use of market segmentation to select and address a key group of potential purchasers.

Unique Selling Proposition (USP) – the benefit that a product or service can deliver to customers that is not offered by any competitors.

Unit contribution – see contribution.

Variable costs – costs that vary according to the level of activity or sales.

Variance – the difference between a planned or budgeted activity and the actual cost or result. A variance may be positive (or favourable) or negative (or adverse). Variance analysis is used to assess performance and identify when corrective action is required.

Vision – the long-term aims and aspirations of the company for itself.

Word of mouth – the spreading of information through human interaction alone.

Appendix 1

Feedback to Case Studies

Session 1

1. **Metro used marketing research to inform various stages of its' marketing plan. From the Case Study identify three reasons why research was used.**

    To discover:

    a. What newspapers London's tube commuters were reading.

    b. What the profile of current readers was.

    c. What the potential market size and make up for a national version of their paper might be.

2. **Explain how each of the three types of research identified in 1. (above) might be collected.**

    a. Face-to-face survey at tube stations or observation.

    b. Analysis of data held, or secondary data from the Census for example.

    c. Secondary data held as a result of omnibus surveys perhaps or from national statistics.

3. **The Case Study mentions the fact that Metro is exploring opportunities to move into new markets. Explain two important sources of data that Metro might use for this purpose, justifying your answer.**

    Employment trends (obtainable through national statistics), showing the potential of a particular region.

    International markets – competitor information could be obtained through the Internet, or from government information on the target region.

Session 2

1. **Identify the competitor information that you would want to gather for analysis before making your decision about the new product.**

    What competitors are there in the market to be targeted?

What similar products do they offer?

What interest rates do they offer?

What take up of products have they achieved?

What does their marketing activity comprise of?

How do they reach the market?

2. **Identify sources of internal data that might be useful before making a decision.**

    Records of current customers in these cities.

    Profiles of current customers in these cities.

    Reports of previous research undertaken.

    Customers with investment products that are maturing, and would qualify for the new scheme.

3. **List the concerns that you have about the research commissioned by your predecessor.**

    Focus groups only, and very few of these.

    Not a representative sample – i.e. only MBA students.

    Only two of the three locations researched.

    Research does not take account of other market factors.

Session 3

1. **Explain the term "customer centricity" as it is used in the Case Study.**

    The term is used to describe a customer-focused strategy that places the customer at the centre of all business.

2. **The Case Study stresses that CRM should benefit both parties in the relationship. Identify three benefits that CRM might offer customers.**

    Product and services are designed to meet customers' specific needs.

Ordering is straightforward and customer service is excellent, so it is easier to stay with the organisation practicing CRM than to move to another organisation.

Communications would be relevant and a "dialogue" established.

3. **The Case Study talks about protecting the privacy of customers. Identify any legislation in your country that exists to protect this privacy.**

This will vary from country to country. In the UK it is protected by the Data Protection Act (1998).

Session 4

1. **The Case Study talks about splitting the database into "front-end" and "back-end" operations. Explain the difference between the two systems.**

Front-end systems are sales, marketing, and customer service related, and usually involve data being input onto "forms" (easy-to-use computer screens that allow the input of data for instance). As the Case Study states, these are the revenue earning systems.

Back-end systems are those such as finance, ordering, and production systems, which, when integrated with the front-end systems, produce more powerful data.

2. **Explain what is meant by the term "customer insight".**

Customer insight is the term used for the depth of understanding possible through combining aggregated marketing research information into an existing database of customer information.

3. **The Case Study argues for the "completeness" of data (detail and relevancy), and mentions adding a "SIC" code for business-to-business marketing. How might this benefit the company using the database?**

The SIC code is a Standard Industry Classification, and will provide an extra category by which customers can be profiled. This will allow them to examine records and see if any industry is more profitable, spends more, buys greater volume, etc. This will allow them to adjust any key account strategy, employ people with relevant knowledge, and target other companies in the sector.

Session 5

1. **Advise Mike of the different types of market research practitioners that could help him.**

   - Specialist agencies – either in terms of industry or type of study undertaken.
   - Full service.
   - Consultants.
   - Fieldwork agencies.
   - Analytical specialists.

2. **Make a recommendation as to the factors he should consider when selecting the most suitable type of agency.**

   Factors for consideration:

   - Previous experience of working in the bakery industry may define the need for a specialist agency.
   - Broad range of research needed – may dictate a full-service agency.
   - Budget available – may need to look for a consultant who will offer an appropriate service at a reasonable cost.

3. **Explain to Mike the various stages in the marketing research process, ensuring that he understands the importance of each stage.**

   1. Define the research problem. This stage can help assess whether expensive research is justified, and also help put a brief together.

   2. Set the objectives for the research. Helps ensure that results are valid and reliable.

   3. Construct the research proposal. This ensures that there is full agreement on how the research will progress and how much it might cost.

   4. Specify data collection methodology. How the data will be collected.

   5. Select the sample. It is extremely rare that marketers can afford to research the whole of the relevant population, so accurate sampling is incredibly important and can make the difference between the success or failure of the research.

6. Undertake some preliminary desk research.

7. Define the questions to be asked. Design the questionnaire and pilot.

8. Collect the data. The action stage of the process.

9. Analyse and interpret the findings of the research.

10. Present the results. Once sense has been made of the data collected, it then needs to be presented in a suitable format for the users of the research. This is often a formal report and a presentation with a question and answer session.

Session 6

1. **In the last Session you advised Mike on how he should decide on which type of marketing research practitioner to use. Now advise him on the other factors he will need to consider before selecting an agency.**

    ■ Their interpretation of the brief and translation into an appropriate proposal.

    ■ The compatibility of the staff of the two organisations, as they will need to develop a working relationship.

    ■ Demonstration of a real understanding of the problems Cromwell's are facing.

    ■ Their experience in the geographical area.

    ■ Evidence of a creative approach to the problem.

    ■ Suitable methodology recommended.

    ■ Able to meet timescales.

    ■ Price appropriate for budget allocated.

2. **Define the research problem that Cromwell's faces.**

    Cromwell needs information about the speciality bread market:

    Growth rate.
    Market size.
    Competitors and their relative market share.
    Who are the customers?
    What is the Decision-Making Unit (DMU)?

Also, it needs to know what brand awareness levels it has, and what the perceived image of the company is by its customers and the trade.

3. **Write a research brief for Cromwell's current research needs.**

Background

Cromwell Breads are disappointed with sales of their speciality bread. This is a high-margin product in a growth sector and they therefore wish to reverse the trend.

To do so they need to make decisions about promotion, pricing, distribution channels and the positioning of the product.

Objectives

To forecast the demand for speciality bread in the UK.

To identify potential new distribution channels in the UK.

To map the structure of the market for speciality bread.

Information needs

Growth rate.
Market size.
Competitors and their relative market share.
Who are the customers?
What is the DMU?

Methodology

1. Desk research will establish what statistics and information is available for market size and growth rate in the UK, the purchasing patterns for speciality bread, competitive data, and other information related to the objectives.

2. Field research will include visits to retailers in the UK to establish prices at the point of sale of the most popular brands identified in the competitor research.

3. Consumer research will be carried out with random samples of 20 individuals in each target region to identify buying criteria, habits and attitudes.

Timetable

Phase 1:   Desk research (March and April).
Phase 2:   Field research in three target UK regions (May and June).
Phase 3:   Focus groups in three target UK regions (July).
Phase 4:   Report writing and presentation of results (August).

Budget

Preliminary research – £x
Field research – £x
Focus groups – £x
Reporting – £x

Session 7

1. **Identify any further questions you would want to ask the company before preparing the proposal.**

   ### Background and rationale

   Are details available from the database of the profiles of existing key accounts and of other customers?

   ### Objectives

   What specifically are they looking to find out about purchase behaviour?

   ### Method and sample

   No further questions.

   ### Reporting and presentation requirements

   What will be required?

   ### Timing

   When do they need the results of the research?

2. Prepare a proposal in response to the brief from Belts and Braces.

Proposal for Belts and Braces

1. Background to the project

Background information of relevance to the project can be summarised as follows:

a. Belts and Braces manufactures belts for the clothing industry.

b. The company's products are supplied to many of the UK's largest retailers, although recently there has been a strong dependence on one major key account.

c. In order to lessen its dependence on a relatively limited customer base and to identify new segments for its products, the company is considering entry into the UK market for retail belts.

d. In order to assist the company, a programme of marketing research is required that will:

- Evaluate the potential that exists in the retail belt market.
- Identify the segments of the market that offer the best potential.
- Identify the critical success factors necessary to secure a share of this market.

2. Research objectives

Given this background to the project, the objectives of the research programme can be summarised as follows:

a. To quantify the approximate size of the market for retail garment belts.

b. To quantify the structure of the market with respect to factors such as:

- Pricing levels.
- Material type.
- Seasonality (if any) in purchasing.

c. To assess the structure of distribution for retail garment belts with respect to:

The relative importance of alternative sources of retail distribution, such as:

- Department stores.
- Fashion retailers.
- Mail order.
- Leather/specialist stores.
- Other.

The structure of distribution, for example:

- Direct sales to retailers.
- Sales via wholesalers or intermediates.

d. To profile the pricing, margin and mark-up structure at each level in the distribution chain.

e. To evaluate the climate of competition that exists in the market with respect to:

- Major UK/foreign suppliers to the market; approximate estimates of market shares.
- Perceptions of their strengths and weaknesses.
- Factors favouring/not favouring a new market entrant.

f. To identify the key criteria adopted by retail buyers and consumers when evaluating potential suppliers of garment belts, for example:

- Price.
- Product range.
- Style.
- Material.
- Availability.
- Quality.
- Marketing/promotional support.

g. To identify the type and nature of the promotional activity required to support a supplier of branded retail belts.

3. Recommended approach

In order to meet the objectives of the research programme, it is proposed that the research should be undertaken in two stages as follows:

Stage One – assessment of the market for retail belts.

Stage One of the research programme will essentially be concerned with:

- Assessing the structure and dynamics of the market.
- Identifying the sectors of the market that may offer the potential for development by Belts and Braces.

This stage of the research will also consider:

- Key trends in the market.
- Competitor evaluation.
- Pricing levels.
- Distribution channels.
- Retail buyer's purchasing criteria.
- Retail buyer's purchasing practices.

Stage Two – consumer purchasing behaviour

Stage One of the research programme will have assisted in identifying the sectors of the market that may offer the potential for development by Belts and Braces.

The main purpose of Stage Two is to obtain insight into purchasing behaviour with respect to:

- Reasons for purchase (e.g. own purchase, gift).
- Key factors governing choice of retailer selected.
- Key factors governing choice of belt selected.

4. Research method

The research programme will be undertaken by means of the following inputs:

4.1 Project planning

An initial meeting will be held with Belts and Braces for the purposes of:

- Obtaining further information on the company and its products.
- Reviewing any market information already held by the company.
- Confirming the objectives and scope of the research project.
- Clarifying any outstanding points on the project.

4.2 Desk research

An intensive phase of desk research will subsequently be undertaken to locate all relevant information on the market.

This will include a review of relevant information on the garment industry and the structure of retail distribution.

A number of sources will be used, namely:

- Trade magazines.
- Trade associations.
- Market and industry reports.
- Government statistics, including imports and exports.

4.3 Retailer interviewing programme

Following the desk research, a topic guide will be developed in line with the objectives of the project.

The main part of the project will comprise of a programme of personal and telephone interviews with the management responsible for buying belts amongst principal retailers. Subject to the findings of the desk research, it is envisaged that the following interviews will be undertaken:

Department stores: 8
Fashion retailers: 8
Mail order: 5
Leather/specialist outlets: 10
Others: 5

Of these, it is envisaged that six interviews will be carried out on a face-to-face basis; the remainder will be undertaken by telephone.

The emphasis will be directed towards the larger retailers in the market.

4.4 Consumer research programme

In order to obtain some insight into consumer purchasing behaviour and buying criteria it is proposed to carry out a programme of 20 face-to-face interviews with consumer buyers of belts.

Key inputs to this stage of the research will be as follows:

- Interviews will be carried out with people who have recently purchased belts, and will be carried out by means of exit interviews (as they leave the store).
- Each interview will last for about 10-15 minutes on average.
- The interviews will be in the form of a semi-structured questionnaire.

4.5 Analysis and presentation procedures

On completion of the research programme, the findings will be presented in the form of a detailed written project.

5. Timing and cost

5.1 Timing

The research programme will take up to three months from initiation to completion.

5.2 Cost

The cost of the research programme as set out in this document will be £X, which is inclusive of all fees and expenses. Any costs incurred in travelling will be charged extra.

Invoicing will comprise 50% on initiation and 50% on completion.

Terms of payment are strictly 30 days net.

Session 8

Use the notes above to identify the reason that Joe used:

1. Each location.

Location	Information needs
British Library.	To access Barbour Index Directory and get contact details for the Architects Association. Also Exhibition Bulletin.
National Statistics Office.	Import and export data.
Internet.	Financial information about the five key players in the market. Prices and industry trends.
Building Centre.	Company catalogues to find technical data.

2. Each publication.

Publication	Information needs
Barbour Index Directory.	Contact details for Architects Association.
Exhibition Bulletin.	Recent and relevant exhibitions and trade shows.
BRAD	Details of trade journals.
Willings Press Guide.	Name of main trade journal to find out recent projects involving the product.
Directory of Associations.	To find contact details for Royal Institute of British Architects.
Directory of Special Libraries and Information Centres.	To find details of The Building Centre.
Building Trade Directory.	Companies to contact.
Findex – directory of market studies.	Market studies.

3. **Each organisation.**

Organisation	Information needs
Architects Association.	Names of companies specifying the product.
Royal Institute of British Architects.	List of organisations to contact.
Stockbrokers.	Financial information about the five key players in the market.
Banks.	Recent economic data.

Explain what part of his information needs each might be used to satisfy.

Session 9

1. **What are the main forms of primary research mentioned in the Case Study? What methods are used to collect the data?**

   Customer satisfaction surveys – collected by telephone and by email.

   Clubcard data is analysed for shopping behaviour and customer profiles.

2. **Suggest further research that would be useful to Tesco in launching and maintaining their online service.**

   PC usage in the UK.

   Questionnaires or focus groups with customers to identify the service they would like to see.

   Existing statistics on Internet buying behaviour.

3. **The Case Study mentions that Tesco analyse data that they obtain from their Clubcard. What advantages does this data offer them?**

   It can provide useful information about customer purchase behaviour, which can be analysed by target segment and geo-demographics.

Session 10

1. **Ethnography/observation is put forward as an alternative to running focus groups. Compare the two methods, identifying the advantages observation might offer over focus groups.**

Ethnography	Focus groups
Provides a more in-depth picture of actual behaviour, rather than what individuals say they will do.	Individuals may say that they will act in a certain way because of influences from other members of the group.
Can be used to "feed in" to the focus group process, specifying areas for discussion.	Focus groups can try to identify reasons for observed behaviour after the event.

2. **Identify from the Case Study the key outputs that are generated through ethnographic "encounters" and suggest how each might be of value to a marketer.**

   Outputs include:

   ■ Field notes – might be used to record shoppers movements in a store for example, and so be useful in designing layout and merchandising displays.

   ■ Case studies – might be a write-up of a period of observation of TV viewing for example.

   ■ Diaries – record patterns of behaviour, for example family purchasing behaviour over a period of time.

   ■ Videos – might be used to observe children's play behaviour with a new product in a range of toys for example.

3. **Ethnographers in the Case Study 'took the number 73 bus and watched how passengers used their mobile phones'. How might marketers have used the results of such a survey?**

   Information about product usage:

   ■ Were passengers using "hands-free" phones? Help with development of accessories.

- Were they being used to listen to the radio? Help with development of services.
- Did phones ring? Help with development of products, ring tones etc.

Session 11

1. What type of follow-up research would you suggest and why?

The research undertaken was quantitative in nature – i.e. it measured the number of current users of the type of information, and what percentage would be prepared to pay a particular price for example. This should be followed up with some qualitative research to find out what respondents might want from the proposed service. Why do they use their current source? What is good about their current source? What is bad about it? How could it be improved to help them?

2. Explain and give an example of when qualitative research should precede a quantitative survey.

One example of when qualitative research should be carried out before quantitative research is when an expert view is required to help shape future quantitative surveys. In this case, in-depth interviews may precede a questionnaire design. An example of this process is when a window manufacturer considers producing a new design for frames for office blocks. Depth interviews might be initially carried out with a small number of architects to explore the general concept, and then a questionnaire designed to assess what interest there is in the proposed product.

3. Explain and give an example of when a qualitative survey might be undertaken following a quantitative survey.

One example of when qualitative research may be carried out after quantitative research is when an organisation is considering opening a new retail outlet in a particular neighbourhood. In this case, foot traffic may be measured first, to gauge the general potential, and then face-to-face surveys might be used to obtain individuals' perception of the brand.

Session 12

1. Design a short questionnaire to use to assess prompted awareness of Cromwell's Bread in face-to-face street interviews outside supermarkets, before undertaking an advertising campaign.

Normally, unprompted awareness would be the type of study undertaken prior to and following an advertising campaign. This task is set to highlight the difference in the questions asked before and after an advertising campaign.

SECTION 1: PERSONAL INFORMATION

1. Name:...
   (You may remain anonymous if you wish)

2. What is your postcode?..

3. Gender: (do not ask!)

   ❑ Male   ❑ Female

4. What is your age?

   ❑ 18-25   ❑ 26-35
   ❑ 36-45   ❑ 46+

5. Who in your family purchases bread?

   ❑ You   ❑ Your partner   ❑ Either of you

6. What is your marital status?

   ❑ Married   ❑ Single

7. Do you have children?

   ❑ Yes   ❑ No

SECTION 2: AWARENESS

8. I am going to read out a list of brand names relating to bread.
   Please answer yes or no, depending on whether you have heard of the brand.

	Yes	No
Landers	.....	.....
Cromwell's	.....	.....
Nimble	.....	.....
Wonderloaf	.....	.....
Weight Watchers	.....	.....

Kingsmill	.....	.....
Hovis	.....	.....
Mother's Pride	.....	.....
Happy	.....	.....
Warburton's	.....	.....

2. **Design a short questionnaire to use as an alternative to the above to assess unprompted awareness of Cromwell's Bread in face-to-face interviews outside supermarkets in Shropshire and Yorkshire.**

    Normally, unprompted awareness would be measured prior to and following an advertising campaign. This question suggests that it is to be carried out in two different regions (Cromwell's home region and one it supplies in another part of the UK). This will allow comparison in awareness levels.

    ### SECTION 1: PERSONAL INFORMATION

    1. Name: ....
        (You may remain anonymous if you wish)

    2. What is your postcode?...

    3. Gender (do not ask!)

        ❏   Male   ❏   Female

    4. What is your age?

        ❏   18-25   ❏   26-35
        ❏   36-45   ❏   46+

    5. Who in your family purchases bread?

        ❏   You   ❏   Your partner   ❏   Either of you

    6. What is your marital status?

        ❏   Married   ❏   Single

    7. Do you have children?

        ❏   Yes   ❏   No

SECTION 2: AWARENESS

8. Can you name five brands of bread?

....

....

....

....

....

3. **Design a discussion guide for a focus group to explore the main influences in the family buying unit as to what sort of bread is purchased and what brand is bought.**

Introductions

Tell me a bit about yourself and your background.
What is your family unit?
Are you in paid employment or not?
Where do you shop for groceries? Why there?

Bread products

Do you buy speciality breads?
Why/Why not?
Which types of speciality breads do you buy?

Patterns of use

What is your typical, daily pattern of bread eating?
What brand of bread did you buy last? Where did you buy it? Why that brand?
Which type of bread do you prefer (fresh baked, pre-packed, part baked, bread mixes)? When do you use the different types? Why?

On which occasions do you use bread? Breakfast? Mid a.m.? Lunch? Afternoon? Dinner? Dinner party?

When eating out, what type of bread do you choose?

Awareness of types

Are you loyal to one type of bread or do you experiment with different types? Which "types" do you know?

How important are the following?

Appearance.
Texture.
Flavour.
Colour.
Price.
Brand.
Packaging.

Session 13

Taking into account the intended survey design, the identified key target respondents, and the indicated budget (as set out in the Case Study), what would be your proposed sample sizes? What is your reasoning for how you would conduct the research for items 1-6 of the survey design?

Budget – £4,000.

One of the main points to bear in mind is that an important element in determining sample size is what variance you expect to find in the target population (the more differentiated the behaviour, the larger the sample required).

1. Desk research to find information on the success of other exhibitions and to find out what media coverage last year's events received.

2. Discussions with last year's organisers should ideally include a number of departments that were involved with the exhibition – from administration, marketing and sales for example. Thus 3-5 individual depth interviews may be conducted.

3. About 2-5 interviews with journalists would give some useful insight into their perceptions of the event and any likely interest in future events.

4. There are 240 exhibitors. In business-to-business research 20-40 interviews within a reasonably "cohesive" group, would typically produce a comprehensive picture. In this instance it is suggested that 20 telephone depth interviews would yield a useful profile. The cost is therefore £600.

5. To extend the coverage of exhibitors' views, might conduct a further 60 interviews in order to identify any distinctions in patterns of behaviour (cost of 60 short telephone interviews @ £10 each = £600).

6. There are seven "categories" of attendee, but since one is "other" it is likely to be very fragmented, so there is little use in trying to profile it as a whole. For the six remaining categories, the main question to ask is whether there are significant sub-sets within those groups, e.g. independent companies versus plcs, or small and medium companies versus large organisations, or local companies versus national or international companies. You could also consider the average size of stand (= revenue generated). The more sub-sets you want to profile, the greater the sample size. For the £2,800 budget that remains, you could conduct 280 interviews. They can be allocated very approximately pro-rata so that of the 10,000 companies, 1,072 were software developers/support companies, so they should have roughly 10% of the interviews. The possible composition could therefore be:

	Number of interviews		Number of interviews
Dealers.	30	Software developer/support companies.	30
Architects and design consultants.	50	VARs.	50
Retailers.	50	Business users.	50

The final consideration is that if you believed that there was more diversity among business users than among the other categories, you could increase that category to 70 interviews with the £200 that remains in the budget.

Session 14

1. **What would you suggest as possible headings for reporting back on the above research?**

   - Title page.
   - Table of contents.
   - Executive summary.

- Problem definition.
- Research method.
- Research findings:
  - Expectations.
  - Needs.
  - Likely reactions.
- Conclusions and recommendations.
- Appendices.

2. **What kind of evidence would provide convincing data for the client?**

   a. Summary of analysis of transcripts from focus groups, grouped under headings taken from the research objectives:

   - Expectations.
   - Needs.
   - Likely reactions.

   b. If recordings have made of the focus groups, actual clips of respondents making relevant statements would also be useful in the presentation of results. In the report quotes could be used.

   c. Clear conclusions drawn from the patterns or trends that emerge from the analysis.

3. **Would you describe the research as exploratory, explanatory or confirming a hypothesis?**

   This is exploratory research.

Session 15

1. **Based on the details provided, what action points would you suggest?**

   Action points might include:

   - Implement promotional mix as recommended.
   - Review the use of the web site to communicate with the various categories of membership, and promote "communities" for interaction and peer-to-peer support.
   - Arrange meetings to make decisions about the implementation of the other recommendations.

- Instigate policy of following up membership lapses.
- Carry out further research into the perception of pricing policy.

2. **How would you summarise the Strengths, Weaknesses, Opportunities and Threats facing the client (as revealed by the research)?**

STRENGTHS	WEAKNESSES
No overt dissatisfaction. Many services of interest. Lack of funding recognised as a constraint.	Low profile with existing members. Lack of knowledge of membership benefits.
OPPORTUNITIES	**THREATS**
Communications plan. Use of web site to support. Introduce specific services and support for different categories of membership.	Lapse of further members. Move to other organisations.

3. **Draw up three slides for a presentation to summarise the findings and evaluation.**

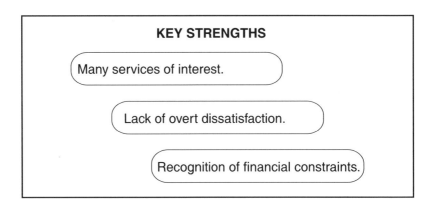

KEY STRENGTHS

Many services of interest.

Lack of overt dissatisfaction.

Recognition of financial constraints.

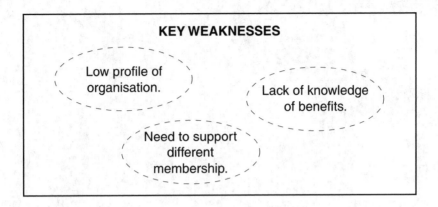

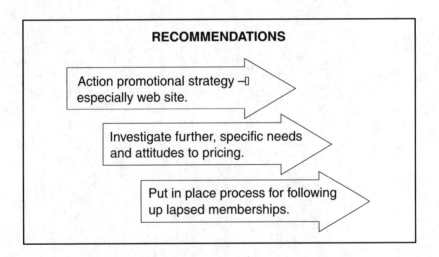

Appendix 2

Syllabus

Aim

The Marketing Research and Information module covers the management of customer information and research projects as part of the marketing process. It provides participants with both the knowledge and skills to manage marketing information and the more specialist knowledge and skills required to plan, undertake, and present results from market research.

This module is a joint syllabus, shared with the Market Research Society.

Related statements of practice:

Ac.1 Identify information requirements and manage research projects and the MkIS.

Ac.2 Evaluate and present information for business advantage.

Bc.1 Contribute information and ideas to the strategy process.

Learning outcomes

Participants will be able to:

- Identify appropriate marketing information and marketing research requirements for business decision-making.

- Plan for and manage the acquisition, storage, retrieval and reporting of information on the organisation's market and customers.

- Explain the process involved in purchasing market research and the development of effective client-supplier relationships.

- Write a research brief to meet the requirements of an organisation to support a specific plan or business decision.

- Develop a research proposal to fulfil a given research brief.

- Evaluate the appropriateness of different qualitative and quantitative research methodologies to meet different research situations.

- Design and plan a research programme.

- Design a questionnaire and discussion guide.

- Interpret quantitative and qualitative data and present coherent and appropriate recommendations that lead to effective marketing and business decisions.

- Critically evaluate the outcomes and quality of a research project.

- Explain the legal, regulatory, ethical and social responsibilities of organisations involved in gathering, holding and using information.

Knowledge and skill requirements

Element 1: Information and research for decision making (15%)

1.1 Demonstrate a broad appreciation of the need for information in marketing management and its role in the overall marketing process.

1.2 Explain the concept of knowledge management and its importance in a knowledge-based economy.

1.3 Explain how organisations determine their marketing information requirements and the key elements of user specifications for information.

1.4 Demonstrate an understanding of marketing management support systems and their different formats and components.

Element 2: Customer databases (15%)

2.1 Demonstrate an understanding of the application and role of Customer Relationship Management (CRM) and the benefits of customer databases.

2.2 Describe the process for setting up a database.

2.3 Explain how organisations profile customers and prospects.

2.4 Explain the principles of data warehouses, data marts and data mining.

2.5 Explain the relationship between database marketing and marketing research.

Element 3: Marketing research in context (25%)

3.1 Describe the nature and structure of the market research industry.

3.2 Explain the stages of the market research process.

3.3 Describe the procedures for selecting a market research supplier.

3.4 Identify information requirements to support a specific business decision in an organisation and develop a research brief to meet those requirements.

3.5 Develop a research proposal to fulfil a given research brief.

3.6 Explain the ethical and social responsibilities inherent in the market research task.

Element 4: Research methodologies (30%)

4.1 Explain the uses, benefits and limitations of secondary data.

4.2 Recognise the key sources of primary and secondary data.

4.3 Describe and compare the various procedures for observing behaviour.

4.4 Describe and compare the various methods for collecting qualitative and quantitative data.

4.5 Design a questionnaire and discussion guide to meet a project's research objectives.

4.6 Explain the theory and processes involved in sampling.

Element 5: Presenting and evaluating information to develop business advantage (15%)

5.1 Demonstrate an ability to use techniques for analysing qualitative and quantitative data.

5.2 Write a research report aimed at supporting marketing decisions.

5.3 Plan and design an oral presentation of market research results.

5.4 Use research and data to produce actionable recommendations for a marketing plan or to support a business decision.

Appendix 3

The Chartered
Institute of Marketing

CIM Professional Series Stage 2

Marketing Research and Information

Marketing Research and Information

Time:

Date:

3 Hours Duration

This examination is in two sections.

PART A – Is compulsory and worth 50% of total marks.

PART B – Has **FOUR** questions; select **TWO**. Each answer will be worth 25% of the total marks.

DO NOT repeat the question in your answer, but show clearly the number of the question attempted on the appropriate pages of the answer book.

Rough workings should be included in the answer book and ruled through after use.

© The Chartered Institute of Marketing

CIM Professional Series
Stage 2

Marketing Research and Information – Specimen Paper

PART A

Donaldson Builders Merchants

Donaldson Builders Merchants is a small chain of builders merchants located in the central belt of Scotland. The company has four outlets located around the edge of the major conurbations of Edinburgh and Glasgow. These supply small builders, plumbers, roofers, and similar tradesmen, as well as some members of the public (i.e. those more skilled in major do-it-yourself renovations and house improvements). Customers may collect items direct from the trade counter at the warehouse or can have the items delivered direct to the building site or house by the company's fleet of 14 lorries. The lorries are equipped with hoists for handling the larger items.

Donaldson supplies:

- Timber and Timber Products.

- Bricks and Paving.

- Sand and Aggregates.

- Roofing Materials.

- Plumbing and Heating Supplies.

- A small range of Hand Tools.

The company provides credit to the majority of its trade customers. As a result it has a computerised database with details on most of its trade customers relating to name, trading address, telephone number, type of business and purchasing patterns. There are approximately 1,100 customers on the database, which probably represent around 85% of the company's customers. For the other 15% of customers (the public and trade customers who don't have a credit account), the database holds no record, with the exception of a delivery address if delivery is required.

The market in which Donaldson operates is becoming more competitive, with the company losing share to national chains such as Jewson and a number of recently opened B&Q trade depots. Tom Donaldson, the Managing Director, feels that the company's personal service and flexibility is far superior to these competitors, and is therefore keen to build on this and find ways in which to compete other than on price. The company has never undertaken research before but is keen to find out more from its customers about:

- Their existing and future purchasing behaviour.

- Their attitudes towards Donaldson Builders Merchants (such as product range, service, flexibility of delivery, etc.).

- Their suggestions about improvements required in Donaldson's offering.

They are willing to spend up to £50,000 on the research project.

PART A

Question 1.

You are a Director of a market research agency and have been asked to:

a.   Identify any further information that you would require from Tom Donaldson prior to writing a proposal.

(10 marks)

b.   Having made reasonable assumptions regarding the answers to the information required in Question 1a., produce a short 3-5 page proposal to address the needs of Tom Donaldson. (For the purpose of this question, your proposal should exclude the sections relating to Personal CVs, Related Experience and References and Contract Details).

(40 marks)
(50 marks in total)

PART B – Answer TWO Questions Only

Question 2.

Tom Donaldson in Question 1. is keen to make more use of his company's database and turn it into a customer database for marketing intelligence and customer relationship purposes. He has asked you as a newly qualified Marketing Executive within the firm to produce a report which sets out:

a.　The benefits and weaknesses of database information to a company such as Donaldson Builders Merchants.

(7 marks)

b.　The manner in which data should be stored and processed for it to be of most use in the provision of marketing intelligence and customer relationship activity.

(9 marks)

c.　The need for the distinction between marketing research and the creation of databases for direct marketing purposes.

(9 marks)
(25 marks in total)

Question 3.

Design a questionnaire to meet the research objectives of the project set out in Question 1. At this stage the layout of the questionnaire is not important, but the questionnaire should clearly demonstrate your knowledge of sequencing, question wording and question/response format.

(25 marks)

Question 4.

As Mr Donaldson in Question 1. has never undertaken research before, he needs guidance in his selection of an agency to undertake the research. He has received proposals from three agencies and he has asked you as an old friend who has used agencies in the past to provide a report on:

a.　The selection criteria to use in determining the successful agency.

(15 marks)

b.　The elements of the professional codes of marketing and social research practice that relate to the relationships between researchers and clients.

(10 marks)
(25 marks in total)

Question 5.

As one of the Director's in the agency that has been awarded the contract for doing the research for Donaldson Builders Merchants in Question 1., you are writing a memorandum to your staff to prepare them for the presentation and evaluation of information at the end of any project. The memorandum should include the following:

a.   An explanation of two approaches that can be used to analyse transcripts from a series of group discussions.

(10 marks)

b.   An explanation of the importance of an understanding of the audience's thinking sequence to the preparation of the final report.

(15 marks)
(25 marks in total)

Appendix 4

Specimen answers

The following do not represent full specimen answers to the specimen examination paper, but instead look at:

- The rationale for the question – what the examiner is looking for.

- The best way to structure your answer.

- The key points that you should have included and expanded upon.

- The main syllabus area that is being assessed.

Please note that many of the key points are represented here in the form of bullet point lists. All of these points should be expanded upon in your answer, unless the examiner **specifically** asks for a bullet-point list.

The timings given for each part of each question allow a little time for reading the Case Study, planning your answers, and choosing which questions you will answer. Remember to follow the instructions on the paper.

If you studied for the CIM Professional Series Stage 1 (Certificate Level), you will notice that there is a difference in structure between the exam papers at the two levels. The Stage 2 (Advanced Certificate) papers still consist of two sections, but Part A is compulsory and now attracts **50%** of the marks, and Part B requires you to **choose 2 questions from 4**, each of which attracts **25%** of the marks.

Part A

Question 1.

The Case Study for this paper tests your knowledge of all aspects of the syllabus. It is set in the context of a small chain of builders merchants who are facing a more competitive market, and wish to find out more about their customers. It puts you in the role of a market research agency director.

The important thing to remember about approaching the mini-case question is that you must apply the **concepts** that the examiner is looking for to the **context** and situation described in the case and/or question. With every question that is broken up into sections, you also need to consider how marks are spread across the various parts of the question, as this should dictate how much time you allocate to each part.

Question 1a.

This first part of the compulsory question asks you to identify any further information you would need **before** writing a research proposal. This could be structured using the headings from a typical proposal outline as follows:

Background and rationale

Using the database, are there any obvious differences between those customers using credit and those not?
What types of customer are going to competitors?

Objectives

More detail is needed about the general objectives stated, e.g. what specifically do they want to know about purchase behaviour?
Which areas of their offering are they looking to improve?

Method and sample

Who are the decision makers in purchasing companies?
How useful is their database in selecting sample, categorising customers etc.
Is it possible to get access to customers by phone, or when they visit the warehouse?

Reporting and presentation requirements

What kind of report or presentation is required?

Timing

When do they need the results of the research?

There are 10 marks for this question, so you should spend approximately 15 minutes answering it.

Syllabus references – 1.1, 1.3 and 3.4.

Question 1b.

This part of the question asks you to prepare a 3-5 page proposal, and make any necessary assumptions about the answers you would expect to get. Depending on what assumptions you make, your proposal will take on an appropriate form. However, the key points the examiner is looking for are:

Background

A description of the client organisation and its markets and products.
The rationale for the research.

Objectives

Specifically worded.

Approach and method

Appropriate qualitative and quantitative recommendations, taking account of:

- Numbers and types of customers.

- Need to include those not included on the database, as well as those that are.

- Possibility of getting some behavioural information from the database.

- Practical difficulties of contacting busy builders – may be on building sites most of the time.

- Specific attitudinal and behavioural information needed.

- How the information will be collected.

- Sampling arrangements.

Justification of your proposals

Reporting and presentation arrangements.

Timings

Fees – you should make some attempt to estimate the cost of the proposal you are making.

There are 40 marks for this question, so you should spend approximately 60 minutes answering it.

Syllabus references – 3.5, 4.1-4.4 and 4.6.

Part B

Question 2.

This question is set to assess your understanding of the use of a **customer database** for both **intelligence and relationship** purposes.

This time, you are put in the role of a **newly qualified Marketing Executive** within the firm. You are asked to link your answer to the context of the question.

Question 2a.

You are asked for the benefits and weaknesses of database information.

Benefits

- Helps provide information about customer characteristics and buying behaviour.
- Can be used for forecasting and data mining of the above.
- Helps provide figures on value, profitability and length of relationship.
- Can also measure response to marketing communications campaigns, price changes, introduction of new products, etc.

Weaknesses

- Only gives factual information, not the reasons for the behaviour.
- Although it can be used for forecasting trends, it is based on historical data.
- Only shows customer behaviour for Donaldson's customers.

There are 7 marks for this question, so you should spend approximately 10 minutes answering it.

Syllabus reference – 2.1.

Question 2b.

This part of the question focuses on how data should be stored to provide suitable information for making effective decisions around marketing activity and customer relationship activity.

You should stress the need for effective processes for data capture, and explain the following issues:

- Formatting.
- Validation.
- Removing duplicate information.

There are 9 marks for this question, so you should spend approximately 15 minutes answering it.

Syllabus references – 2.1 and 2.2.

Question 2c.

This final part of the question is looking for you to explain the need to keep the use of the database for marketing research purposes and direct marketing purposes separate.

You should explain:

- The need for marketing research respondents to be assured of anonymity and confidentiality.
- The need for transparency.
- The Codes of Conduct in place.
- The need for partly aggregated data to be transferred to the database from marketing research findings.

You should link your explanations to examples based on Donaldson Builders Merchants wherever possible.

There are 9 marks for this question, so you should spend approximately 15 minutes answering it.

Syllabus references – 2.5 and 3.6.

Question 3.

This is a straightforward question asking you to **design a questionnaire** to meet set marketing research objectives. It stresses the need to demonstrate your understanding of **sequencing, question wording, and question/response format** in a practical way.

Your questionnaire should show:

Wording

You need to ensure that all the questions are clear and unambiguous. Check that none of your questions "lead" the respondent to a certain answer. None of your questions should be "multiple" questions – i.e. they should contain only one topic and not try to measure two things at once.

Question/response format

These should be relevant to the objectives that are to be met and the questions being asked. Try to use a range of formats if possible – open-ended, closed, dichotomous, multiple choice, scaling, etc.

Sequencing

The sequence should be logical, and start broad and funnel in.

There are 25 marks for this question, so you should spend approximately 40 minutes answering it.

Syllabus reference – 4.5.

Question 4.

For this question you take on yet another role – that of **knowledgeable friend.** You are asked for your advice in agency selection.

Question 4a.

This part of the question asks you about the **selection criteria** to be used when choosing between three **agencies.** The advantage of using an agency is that they will have the expertise and facilities that you do not have in-house. They are also able to take a more objective view. Once you are down to three, you are in a shortlist situation, so you will already have checked out their expertise and facilities, as well as their financial stability.

In this context the selection criteria should include:

- Interpretation of brief and translation into an appropriate proposal.
- Compatibility of the staff of the two organisations, as they will need to develop a working relationship.
- Previous experience of working in the construction/retail building trade.
- Demonstration of a real understanding of the problems Donaldson's are facing.

- Experience in the geographical area.

- Evidence of a creative approach to the problem.

- Suitable methodology recommended.

- Able to meet timescales.

- Price appropriate for the budget allocated.

There are 15 marks for this question, so you should spend approximately 22 minutes answering it.

Syllabus reference – 3.3.

Question 4b.

This part of the question asks about Codes of Practice, and your answer will relate to your own country's arrangements. The following areas will generally be included in a Code of Conduct, and will usually be included in a written contract:

- Researchers should advise clients if they intend to sub-contract any of the work.

- They should specify that ownership of the brief and specifications, as well as the results, remain the property of the client.

- Proposals and quotes remain the property of the agency.

- Any publication of findings should only be undertaken with the permission of the client and should not be misleading.

- When presenting the report on the results, the agency should differentiate between, findings, interpretation and recommendations.

There are 10 marks for this question, so you should spend approximately 16 minutes answering it.

Syllabus reference – 3.6.

Question 5.

The final question places you back in the role of a **director of the marketing research agency** that has been awarded the contract. It is set to assess your knowledge of **analytical techniques** and **presentation techniques.**

Question 5a.

This part of the question asks you to explain **two** approaches to analysing **transcripts from focus groups**.

These will contain qualitative data, and you could explain any two of the following:

- Tabulation.
- Content analysis software.
- Text analysis software.
- Cut and paste technique.
- Spider-type diagrams.
- Annotation method.

There are 10 marks available for the two approaches, so you should expect 5 marks to be awarded for your explanation of the **strengths and weaknesses** of each of the two approaches you explain.

There are 10 marks for this question, so you should spend approximately 16 minutes answering it.

Syllabus reference – 5.1.

Question 5b.

This final part of the question asks you to explain the importance of understanding the audience's thought process when preparing your report to present the findings.

The thought sequence is:

- **Respect my importance** – make the report professional in appearance, clarity and relevance.
- **Consider my needs** – demonstrate that you understand the original problem, and how important it is to me.
- **Demonstrate how your information helps me** – explain the findings and what they mean to me.
- **Explain the detail behind your information** – use examples, charts and tables to link the objectives to the results.
- **Remind me of the key points** – summarise.

- **Suggest what I should do now** – make clear recommendations.

There are 15 marks for this question, so you should spend approximately 22 minutes answering it.

Syllabus reference – 5.2.

Appendix 5

Assessment guidance

There are two methods used for assessment of candidates – Examination OR Continuous Assessment via projects.

The Chartered Institute of Marketing has traditionally used professional, externally set examinations as the means of assessment for the Certificate, Advanced Certificate and Postgraduate Diploma in Marketing. In 1995, at the request of industry, students and tutors, it introduced a continuously assessed route to two modules, one at Certificate level, and one at Advanced Certificate. With an increased emphasis on marketing practice, all modules at Certificate level are now open to assessment through examination or assessed project.

With the introduction of the CIM Professional Series, all modules are available on a project basis, and decisions about the assessment of Stage 3 will be made shortly.

The information in this appendix will:

- Help you prepare for project-based assessment.

- Provide hints and tips to help you prepare for the examination.

- Manage your time effectively in preparing for assessment.

NB: Your tutor will inform you which method of assessment applies to your programme.

Preparing for project-based assessment

If you are being assessed by project you will be given a full brief for the assignment. This will include what you have to do, how it is to be presented, and the weighting of marks for each section. **YOU MUST READ THIS BEFORE YOU START, AND CHECK YOUR UNDERSTANDING WITH YOUR TUTOR.**

The assignment will consist of a number of tasks, each with their own weighting, so make sure you take account of this in your final presentation of the project.

The size of the project will be identified by a recommended word count. Check your final word count carefully, but remember quality is more important than quantity.

The assignment tasks will include a reflective statement. This requires you to identify what you have learned from the experience of undertaking the module, and how you have applied that learning to your job.

Questions you might want to consider to help you write this reflective statement include: What was the most difficult part? How did you feel at the start of the exercise and how do you feel at the end? Did you achieve your objectives? If not, why not? What have you learned about yourself as you have worked through the module? How much of your learning have you been able to apply at work? Have you been able to solve any real work problems through work you have done in your assignments?

This statement will be personal to you, and it should look forward to the points you have identified as needing work in the future. We never stop learning. You should keep up this process of Continuous Professional Development as you go through your studies and your career, and hopefully you will have acquired the habit by the time you need to employ it to achieve Chartered Marketer status!

Examinations

Each subject differs slightly from the others, and the style of question will differ between module examinations. All are closed book examinations.

For all examinations the examination paper consists of two sections:

Part A – Mini-case, scenario or article

This section has a mini-case, scenario or article with compulsory questions. You are required to make marketing or sales decisions based on the information provided. You will gain credit for the decisions and recommendations you make on the basis of the analysis itself. This is a compulsory section of the paper designed to evaluate your practical marketing skills. This section will attract 50% of the total marks.

Part B – Examination questions

You will have a choice of two questions from four, and when answering those you select, ensure you understand the context of the question. Rough plans for each answer are strongly recommended. Each of these questions attracts 25% of the marks.

The examination for **Marketing Management in Practice** differs in that the compulsory questions and examination questions are all linked to the mini-case and additional relevant information may be given, such as memos and reports.

CIM Code of Conduct for examinations

If being assessed by examination you will receive examination entry details, which will include a leaflet entitled "Rules for Examinations". You should read these carefully, as you will be penalised by CIM if you are in breach of any of these rules.

Most of the rules are common sense. For example, for closed book examinations you are not allowed to take notes or scrap paper into the examination room, and you must use the examination paper supplied to make rough notes and plans for your answer.

Hints and tips

There are a number of places you can access information to help you prepare for your examination, if you are being assessed by this method. Your tutor will give you good advice, and exam hints and tips can also be found on the CIM student web site (www.cimvirtualinstitute.com).

Some fundamental points are listed below.

- Read the question carefully, and think about what is being asked before tackling the answer. The examiners are looking for knowledge, application and context. Refer back to the question to help you put your answer in the appropriate context. Do not just regurgitate theory.

- Consider the presentation style of your answer. For example, if you are asked to write a report, then use a report format with number headings and not an essay style.

- Structure – plan your answer to make it easy for the examiner to see the main points you are making.

- Timing – spread your time in proportion to the marks allocated, and ensure that all required questions are answered.

- Relevant examples – the examiners expect relevant theory to be illustrated by practical examples. These can be drawn from your own experience, reading of current journals and newspapers, or just your own observations. You could visit "Hot Topics" on the CIM student web site to see discussions of topical marketing issues and practice.

Managing your time

What is effective time management? It is using wisely one of your most precious resources, **TIME**, to achieve your key goals. You need to be aware of how you spend your time each day. Set priorities, so you know what's important to you, and what isn't. You need to establish goals for your study, work and family life, and plan how to meet those goals. Through developing these habits you will be better able to achieve the things that are important to you.

When study becomes one of your key goals you may find that, temporarily, something has to be sacrificed in favour of time needed for reading, writing notes, writing up assignments, preparing for group assessment, etc. It helps to "get people on your side". Tell people that you are studying and ask for their support – these include direct family, close friends and colleagues at work.

Time can just slip through your fingers if you don't manage it, and that's wasteful! When you are trying to balance the needs of family, social life, working life and study, there is a temptation to leave assignments until the deadline is nearly upon you. Don't give in to this temptation! Many students complain about the heavy workload towards the end of the course, when, in fact, they have had several months to work on assignments, and they have created this heavy workload themselves.

Knowing how to manage your time wisely can help you:

- Reduce pressure when you're faced with deadlines or a heavy schedule.
- Be more in control of your life by making better decisions about how to use your time.
- Feel better about yourself because you're using your full potential to achieve.
- Have more energy for things you want or need to accomplish.
- Succeed more easily because you know what you want to do and what you need to do to achieve it.

Finally…

Remember to continue to apply your new skills within your job. Study and learning that is not applied just wastes your time, effort and money! Good luck with your studies!

Index

See also the Glossary on page 219.

You may find referring back to the Learning Outcomes and the Summary of Key Points at the beginning and end of each Session will aid effective use of the Index.

Only where subjects are relevantly discussed or defined are they indexed.